Our Daily Bread

Francisco Candido Xavier

Our Daily Bread

Dictated by the spirit
Emmanuel

ISBN: 978-85-7945-036-5
Original title in Portuguese:
PÃO NOSSO
Brazil, 1950

Translated by: Darrel W. Kimble and Ily Reis

Cover design by: Evelyn Yuri Furuta e Rones José Silvano de Lima

Layout: Rones José Silvano de Lima

Edition of
INTERNATIONAL SPIRITIST COUNCIL
SGAN Q. 909 – Conjunto F
70790-090 – Brasilia (DF) – Brazil
www.edicei.com
edicei@edicei.com
+55 61 3038-8400
Sales: + 55 61 3038 8425

Second Edition 8/2011

Authorized edition by Brazilian Spiritist Federation

INTERNATIONAL DATA FOR CATALOGING IN PUBLICATION (ICP)

E46r Emmanuel (Spirit).

Our daily bread / dictated by the spirit Emmanuel ; [received by] Francisco Cândido Xavier ; translated by Darrel W. Kimble and Ily Reis. – Brasilia (DF), Brazil : International Spiritist Council, 2011.
374 p. ; 21 cm

Original title: Pão nosso.
ISBN 978-85-7945-036-5

1. Spiritualism. 2. Bible and spiritualism. I. Xavier, Francisco Cândido, 1910-2002. II. Title.

CDD 133.9
CDU 133.7

Contents

In Christian Service

For we must all appear before the judgment seat of Christ so that each one may receive according to what he has done while in the body, whether good or evil. – Paul (2 Cor. 5:10)

There is no lack of those who see Spiritism as a mere field of phenomenological experimentation with no moral significance for individuals.

Many students of the Consoling Doctrine thus limit themselves to laboratory investigations or philosophical discussions.

However, it is imperative to realize that there are as many categories of discarnate humans as there are of incarnate ones.

Argumentative, frivolous, rebellious and unstable spirits abound everywhere. Moreover, enigmas and problems arise for the inhabitants of both realms.

In light of this, the discarnate supporters of effective world progress fight for Spiritism with Jesus, turning communication between the two worlds into a factor of sanctified spirituality.

It is our belief that we should not tap into another circle of life if we are not interested in improving our character in the one we inhabit.

There is no value in studying resources that will not edify us.

Thus, for those of us who believe that our hearts have awakened to the responsibilities of living, Spiritism does not represent a mere belief in immortality: it entails service and spiritual growth.

There is no point in believing in the soul's survival after death if one has not prepared oneself for life in the spirit world. And in this effort to ready ourselves we have no wiser and more loving guide than Christ.

Only in the light of his sublime lessons is it possible to readjust our pathway, renew our minds and purify our hearts.

Not everything that is remarkable is divine.

Not everything that is grand is respectable.

Not everything that is beautiful is holy.

Not everything that is pleasant is useful.

The problem is not only to become knowledgeable but to reform ourselves for the expansion of the good.

Therefore, let us cherish the Gospel by living and feeling it, grasping the need for our inner illumination, because, according to the timely and wise words of the Apostle, "… we must all appear before the judgment seat of Christ so that each one may receive according to what he has done while in the body, whether good or evil."

EMMANUEL

Pedro Leopoldo, Brazil February 22, 1950

~ 1 ~

Let's Get to Work

What then shall we do, brothers? When you come together, each one of you has a psalm, a teaching, a revelation, a tongue or an interpretation. Everything is done for edification. – Paul (1 Cor. 14:26)

The church at Corinth was struggling with a number of pressing concerns when Paul wrote the above remark.

The contents of his letter dealt with several spiritual problems facing the Peloponnesian brethren; however, we can isolate this particular verse and apply it to certain situations experienced by new Christian groups formed within the environs of Spiritism's revival of the Gospel.

We very often see intense concern on the part of Spiritist workers for new examples of phenomenology and revelation.

Some groups tend to stop their activities altogether when there are no experienced mediums available.

Why?

No medium can ultimately resolve the fundamental problem of his or her fellow Spiritists' illumination.

Our spiritual task would be absurd if it were circumscribed to the mechanical attendance of a large number of people at any Center simply to emphasize the efforts of only a few.

Disciples must understand that work and accomplishment belong to everyone and that each person must be busy with his or her own spiritually constructive service. No one should complain about a lack of new information when voluminous concessions from the higher realms are awaiting the firm commitment of the willing student who seeks to understand life and to grow spiritually.

When you gather together, remember the doctrine and the revelation, the power to speak and to interpret that you already possess, and get to work for the good and the light in the indispensable pursuit of self-improvement.

~ 2 ~

Think a Little

"The works I do in my Father's name bear witness of me." – Jesus (Jn. 10:25)

The concern of ordinary individuals regarding family traditions and the earthly institutions to which they attach themselves is commonplace, as is their taking pride in the conventional titles that identify who they are as persons.

However, in the life that is real, no one is known by such things. Each spirit brings with it the living history of its own deeds and only the works it has accomplished will reveal each spirit's worth or demerit.

By this we do not mean that words do not have their undeniable advantages; nonetheless, one must understand that words are also a profound potential received from the Infinite Goodness as a divine resource; thus, it is crucial for us to know for certain what we are doing with this gift from the Eternal Lord.

In this respect, Jesus' statement is clothed in imperishable beauty.

What would we say about a Savior who set rules for humankind without having shared in its problems and obstacles?

Christ began his divine mission among peasants; he lived among irascible doctors of the law and rebellious sinners; he associated with the sick and the afflicted; he ate the hard bread of humble fishermen, and finished up his holy work between two thieves.

What are you hoping for? If you are waiting for an easy life and situations of prominence in the world, remember the Master and think a little.

~ 3 ~

The Plough

Jesus said to him, "No one who puts his hand to the plow and looks back is fit for the Kingdom of God." – (Lk. 9:62)

Here, Jesus is utilizing one of the most beautiful symbols for building the Divine Kingdom.

Of course, if the Master had so desired, he could have created other images. He could have alluded to the world's laws, to social obligations or to prophetic texts, but he preferred to rest his teaching on a simpler basis.

The plough is a tool of all time. It is heavy and requires a collaborative effort between man and implement; it causes sweat and requires caution; most of all, it breaks the soil to enable it to produce. It builds a cradle for the seeds, and as it passes, the soil gives way so that the rain, the sun and fertilizers may be properly utilized.

Hence, it is necessary for the sincere disciple to learn from the Divine Cultivator and embrace the plough of responsibility in the spiritually edifying struggle without giving up, thereby avoiding serious harm to the "soil of the self".

Let us ponder the lost opportunities; the showers of mercy which have fallen on us, but which have slipped away without having benefited our spirit; the loving sun which has given us life for many millennia; and the precious fertilizers which we have refused by preferring idleness and indifference.

Let us examine all this and reflect on Jesus' depiction.

A plough promises work, discipline, affliction and fatigue; nonetheless, we must not forget that after the plough come the sowing and the harvest, bread on the table, and full silos.

~ 4 ~

Before Serving

"Just as the Son of Man has come not to be served but to serve." – Jesus (Mt. 20:28)

In the company of the spirit of service, we will always be well watched-over. All of Creation reaffirms this truth with absolute clarity.

From the lowest realms to the highest, all things serve in their own time.

With its divisions and specialized tasks, the law of labor is present in the humblest elements of the diverse sectors of Nature.

For instance, this tree will cure illnesses, while that one will produce fruit. There are stones that contribute to the construction of homes, while others exist to pave roads.

The Father has given his children their planetary home, where every object is in its proper place, merely awaiting the worthy effort and word of command to teach the individual the art of serving. If humans were given gunpowder for the release of energy, and if gunpowder continues to be used as an instrument of death against fellow beings, this is added to the debt of the users of the earthly dwelling, for, in everything, the Supreme Lord suggests the practice of the good, aiming at the elevation and enrichment of all the values of the Universal Patrimony.

Let us not forget that Jesus was always working as he walked among us. Let us examine the nature of the Master's sacrificial cooperation, and learn from him the happiness of faithfully serving.

You can begin this very day.

A hoe or a cooking pot is an excellent starting point. If you are infirm, your hands unable to collaborate directly, you can begin nonetheless by serving in the moral edification of your brothers and sisters.

~5~

Wages

"Be content with your pay." – John the Baptist (Lk. 3:14)

John the Baptist's reply to the soldiers' request for an explanation is a model of concise common sense.

Many people get lost in inextricable mazes due to their deficient understanding about problems of remuneration in everyday life.

There are laborers who demand the wages of ministers of state without pondering the grave responsibilities that often transform world administrators into victims of anxiety and sleeplessness, if not into martyrs of public appearances and banquets.

There are educated individuals who trade tranquility at home for an increase in their salaries.

Countless persons go from youth to old age, anxious and disbelieving, infirm and afflicted, because they are unhappy with the monthly wages that the circumstances of the human pathway have assigned to them within the Unfathomable Designs.

It is not by making a lot of money that individuals will become integrated into the divine circles.

If persons realized that the greater their responsibilities and the more they are paid, the more stressed they will be.

Since ancient times, popular philosophy has stated that the larger the ship the larger the storm. Contentment with his or her own wages is proof of a worker's elevated understanding regarding the justice of the Almighty.

Thus, rather than focusing on the wages of the earth, make it a habit of prizing the gifts of heaven.

~ 6 ~

Make Use of the Light

"Walk while you have the light, so that the darkness does not overtake you." – Jesus (Jn. 12:35)

Meditative persons will encounter divine thoughts as they analyze the past and the future. They will see themselves placed between two eternities – that of the days that have passed and that of the days yet to come.

As they examine the treasures of the present, they will discover their precious opportunities.

In the future, they foresee the blessed light of immortality, whereas in the past, they behold the darkness of their ignorance, the wrongs they committed, and the experiences they handled badly. A crushing majority of people have no other picture regarding the recent or remote past except one comprised of ruin and disenchantment. This compels them to reevaluate the resources at hand.

Thus, in spite of being transitory, human life is the flame that puts you in contact with the work you need to do in order to evolve rightly. By taking advantage of this blessed opportunity, you can learn, attain, accomplish and reunite; you can redeem, correct, reconcile, and enrich yourself in the Lord.

Reflect on the Master's remark and you will grasp its enlightening meaning. "Walk while you have the light," he said.

Take advantage of the gift of time you have received by doing spiritually constructive work.

Lift yourselves from your lower condition by acquiring a higher understanding.

Without the signs of improvement and accomplishment as you go along, you will be dominated by the darkness; that is, you will waste your sacred opportunity by turning to unworthy impulses, and after the death of the body, you will return to the same place of darkness from which you emerged in order to climb new steps on the sublime mountain of life.

~ 7 ~

The Seed

And when you sow, you do not sow the body that shall be, but rather a mere grain of wheat or some other seed. – Paul (1Cor. 15:37)

In the workings of Nature, we see the seed as taking on the sacred role of priestess of the Creator and Life.

The glorious heiress of divine power, it participates in the evolution of the world and silently transmits to the individual its sublime lesson, marked with infinite significance.

It wisely exemplifies the need for starting points, conscientious work demands, proper places, and appropriate times.

There are restless and insatiable persons who have not yet understood the symbol of the seed. They expect great accomplishments from one day to the next. They impose tyrannical measures through the force of orders or weapons, or else they try to cheat the profound laws of Nature. They accelerate the processes of their ambitions, establish temporary domination, boast of fictitious conquests, exalt themselves, and then fall, without any sanctifying accomplishment for themselves or for others.

They have not been able to grasp the lesson of the tiny seed, which provides wheat for their daily bread and guarantees them life in every arena of the planetary struggle.

Knowing how to begin is a very important skill.

In our redemptive effort, we must not lose sight of the smallest possibilities: a gesture, a conversation, an hour of our time, or a word can represent glorious seeds for immortal accomplishments. It is crucial, therefore, never to disregard them.

8

Anxieties

Casting all your anxiety on him, for he cares for you. – (1 Pet. 5:7)

Anxieties trigger many crimes and they never construct anything useful on the earth.

Invariably, hasty persons have all the odds stacked against them.

In contrast to tormenting anxieties, Nature's lessons on patience speak to every sector of the human pathway.

If people were born to be anxious, it would be the same as saying that they have come into the world not as laborers to fulfill a sanctifying task, but as unredeemable souls in despair.

If people would reflect more judiciously, they would recognize the opportunities for service that the moments of each day have to offer, and they would know how to look after their own endowments.

Of course, the scenery changes constantly, compelling us to confront unpleasant surprises as a result of our inappropriate attitude toward happiness or pain. However, our obligation to progress daily toward the good is an essential imperative of the Law.

Anxiety tries to assail generous hearts because earth's pathways hold many dark corners and many problems that are hard to solve. That being the case, let us remember Peter's prescription.

Cast your anxieties about your hopes on Our Heavenly Father, for the Divine Love desires well-being for all of us.

It is right to strongly desire the victory of the Light, to persevere in the search for peace, to discipline ourselves for the union with the higher realms, and to persist in attuning ourselves to the highest spheres. But do not forget that anxiety always precedes the fall.

~ 9 ~

People of Faith

"Therefore, everyone who hears my words and practices them is like the wise man who built his house upon the rock." – Jesus (Mt. 7:24)

In the gallery of venerable people of the faith, great preachers of the Gospel have always been construed as being the greatest expressions of Christianity. However, this has been the case only when these instruments of the truth have not, in fact, forgotten the watchfulness that is crucial for righteous testimony.

It is interesting to note that, of all his disciples, the Master regards most highly those who listen to his teachings and actually put them into practice. From this we may conclude that people of faith are not only those who are prodigious in words and enthusiasm but those who also display attention and goodwill in light of Jesus' teachings, studying their spiritual content in order to apply them in their daily endeavors.

It is comforting to realize that all those involved in the field of evangelical service will progress toward the inner marvels of the faith. Still, we must at all times point out the great worth of sensible persons, who, upon hearing the teachings and counsels of the Good Tidings, carefully attend to the solutions of all the problems of the day or circumstance, without allowing their individual achievements to take place apart from the indispensable Christian foundations.

In all sorts of service, the help of the spoken word is sacred and essential; however, in the lofty endeavor of self-betterment, learners must never forget the sublime value of keeping still at the right time so that prudence may be heard within their soul, guiding their destiny.

~ 10 ~

Fraternal Sentiments

As for fraternal charity, however, you do not need me to write to you, since you yourselves have been taught by God to love one another. – Paul (1 Thes. 4:9)

A strong contradiction that undermines the human contribution to the divine edifice of Christianity is the sectarian tendency that torments multitudes of its followers.

If there were more reflection, if there were more attention to Jesus' teachings, such unwarranted battles would cease forever.

Even today, with the manifestations from the spirit realm in the renewal of the world, individuals and groups appear all the time, asking for formulas from the Other Side so that they may gather together in the arena of pure fraternity.

However, what are enlightened human beings waiting for in order to truly become each others' brothers and sisters?

Many people forget that true solidarity is rare in environments where there is little spirit of service but an overabundance of criticism. Notable institutions fall on hard times and fail due to a lack of mutual help in the area of understanding, work and goodwill.

Is there really a lack of assistance? No.

Every honest and generous endeavor resonates in the highest spheres to attract selfless collaborators.

When an invasion of disharmony assaults institutions of the good, the human agents involved should blame themselves for their lack of commitment or their indifference toward the act of serving. Let no one ask Heaven for special recipes for fraternity because we have the sacred and immutable formula in the words "Love one another."

~ 11 ~

The Good Is Tireless

And you, my brothers, never tire of doing good. – Paul (2 Thes. 3:13)

It is very common to meet people who claim to be tired of practicing the good. However, we must realize that such allegations do not flow from a pure source.

Only those who seek specific, immediate advantages for their individual interests are overcome with fatigue bordering on desperation when they are unable to achieve their selfish purposes.

We must be on our guard when this or that circumstance leads us to ponder the ills that assail us after the good we think we have sown or nurtured.

The sincere disciple is well aware of the fact that Jesus has performed his ministry of love tirelessly ever since the beginning of the planet's formation. Regarding our own personal cases, the Master very often must have felt the thorn of our ingratitude at seeing our retreat before the work of our own illumination. Christ's patience has never become exhausted at observing our willful and criminal detours, and he lovingly corrects us and constructively tolerates our faults, opening his merciful arms to us for renewing endeavors.

If he has supported us and waited for us for so many centuries, why can we not willingly endure a few small disappointments for a few days?

Paul's remark to the Thessalonians is therefore very correct. If we tire of practicing the good, such a disaster will, of course, show that we have not yet been able to eliminate the evil within us.

~ 12 ~

Have You Thought about This?

Knowing that I must soon leave my tabernacle behind, according to what our Lord Jesus Christ has revealed to me. – (2 Pet. 1:14)

If on many occasions the great voices of Christianity have referred to supposed crimes of the flesh, it is necessary to mention the weaknesses of the "self," the spirit per se, without focusing erroneous accusations on the body as if it were playing the role of an implacable tormenter separate from the soul, which would thus be its prisoner and victim.

We notice that Peter called his physical body his tabernacle.

The human body is a conglomeration of agglutinated cells or earthly fluids that have gathered together according to planetary laws, offering the spirit the holy opportunity to learn, value, reform and dignify life.

Like indolent or wicked workers, human beings frequently impute to this useful instrument the evil qualities with which they are assailed. However, the body is a concession of the Divine Mercy so that the soul may prepare itself for its glorious future.

Rather than casting undue accusations at the body, let us reflect on the millennia it took evolution to form this sacred tabernacle.

Have you ever thought about the fact that you are an immortal spirit, which is on the earth for a while and has at its disposal invaluable energies granted by God for the requirements of your endeavor?

Such energies shape your body.

What are you doing with your feet, your hands, your eyes and your brain? Do you know that these powers have been entrusted to you in order for you to honor the Lord through self-enlightenment? Meditate on these questions and sanctify your body, finding in it your divine temple.

~ 13 ~

Necessary Stages

Repent, therefore, and be converted so that your sins may be blotted out and times of refreshing may come from the presence of the Lord. – (Acts 3:19)

Eager believers quite often think that the work of redemption occurs by means of a few conventional procedures, and that with only a certain amount of outward activity they can attain the loftiest titles alongside the Divine Messengers.

Most Roman Catholics expect exemption from difficulties through outward ceremonies; many Protestants believe they are in full communion with heaven just by singing a few hymns, while a large percentage of Spiritists believe they are in the midst of higher revelations just by having attended a few sessions.

All this amounts to worthy preparation, but that is not all there is to it.

There is an inward illuminating effort, without which no one can enter the sanctuary of the Divine Truth.

Peter's words to the popular masses contain the synthesis of the great plan of the essential transformation every person will have to undergo for the happiness of union with Christ. There are indispensable stages for this accomplishment, for no one can reach the eternal light at the top all at once.

Before anything else, the guilty must repent, acknowledge the extent and size of their wrongs, and convert in order to experience the times of refreshing by means of the presence of the Lord within them. Once they have done so, they will be able to build the Divine inner Kingdom.

If you have truly understood the mission of the Gospel, you will know what stage you are at, and you will know what you must do in order to proceed to the next.

~ 14 ~

Pages

But the wisdom that is from above is first of all pure, then peaceable, prudent, gentle, full of mercy and good fruit, without partiality and without hypocrisy. – (Js. 3:17)

Every written page has a soul, and the believer must scrutinize its character. A sincere examination will immediately clarify where it belongs, whether to the circle of the world's destructive activity or to the center of constructive endeavors for the spirit life.

First of all, the reader friend of the truth and the good will analyze its lines in order to evaluate the purity of its content, understanding that if what it says has come from higher sources, he or she will find therein unmistakable signs of peace, prudence, fraternal affability, loving understanding, and good fruit.

However, if the page reflects the subtle poisons of human partiality, such a message has not come from the noblest spheres of life. Even though it may have originated from discarnate, supposedly high order spirits, if the page does not bring forth harmony and fraternal constructiveness, it is merely a reflection of lower order conditions.

Therefore, examine the pages of your daily contact with the thoughts of others, and keep company with those that desire your spiritual growth. You do not need the ones that seem the most brilliant, but the ones that make you a better person.

15

Thoughts

As for the rest, my brothers, everything that is true, everything that is honest, everything that is just, everything that is pure, everything that is lovely, everything that is admirable – if there is anything virtuous and praiseworthy – think on this. – Paul (Phil. 4:8)

All human endeavors are the result of human thoughts. Before anything else, the evil and the good, the ugly and the beautiful lived in the mental fount that produced them in the ongoing activities of life.

The Gospel lays out the generous course for the human mind to renew itself on the paths of higher spirituality, proclaiming the need for such a transformation on the way to the higher realms. It is not only with the intellectual fine points of philosophy that disciples will begin their efforts to accomplish this goal. Renewing one's thoughts is not as easy as it may appear at first glance. It demands a large capacity for self-denial and profound self-control – qualities that humans cannot achieve without work and heartfelt sacrifice. Thus, many servants of Christ just change the words they use, believing that they have reformed their thoughts. However, at recapitulating retentive experiences when circumstances repeat themselves, they once again encounter the same troubles as before because obstacles and darkness have remained in their mind like hidden phantoms.

To think is to create. The manifestation of this creation may not play itself out all at once in the arena of transitory effects, but the object formed by the power of the mind lives in the inner world, demanding special attention for the endeavor of continuity or extinction.

Paul's advice to the Philippians displays sublime content. Disciples who are able to comprehend its profound essence, who heed it each and every day by trying to see the true, honest, just, pure and lovely side of all things, will have discovered the divine formula.

~ 16 ~

Whom Do You Obey?

And being made perfect, he became the source of eternal salvation for all those who obey him. – Paul (Heb. 5:9)

Every individual obeys someone or something.

Nobody is without a purpose.

Even rebelliousness is subject to the correcting forces of life.

People are obeying all the time. However, if they have not yet been able to see their submission as a constructive virtue, it is mostly because they are responding to the lower impulses of their nature, thereby resisting the work of their spiritual growth.

They usually make the obedience that saves them the slavery that condemns them. The Lord established stages along the way; he established the law of self-effort for acquiring what is most valuable in life; and he stipulated that humans would have to accept his designs in order to be truly free. Human beings, however, preferred to hold to their inferior condition, and thus created their own imprisonment. Disciples must carefully examine the arena in which they carry out their endeavors.

Whom do you obey? Do you perchance answer first of all to human vanities or the opinions of others before observing the counsels of the Divine Master?

It is fitting to consider this always, because only when we obey the living teachings of Jesus in everything, can we break the enslavement of the world on behalf of our eternal freedom.

~ 17 ~

Intercession

Brothers, pray for us. – Paul (1 Thes. 5:25)

Many people smile ironically when told about intercessory prayer.

People have become so accustomed to theatrical automatism that they have a hard time understanding the profoundest manifestations of spirituality. Nevertheless, intercessory prayer continues to bestow benefits of unalterable value. It would be incorrect to equate this type of prayer with the flattering incense offered to an earthly monarch in order to win certain favors.

Intercessory prayer is one of the most beautiful acts of fraternity and it entails the emission of beneficial and illuminating energies, which, originating from the sincere spirit, accomplish their intended purpose as a blessed contribution of comfort and strength. However, this does not occur as a favor but as a consequence of just laws. It is hard for people to believe in the influence of invisible thought waves; even so, the space that surrounds them is full of sounds that their physical ears cannot detect. They accept only tangible assistance, but in physical nature itself one can see stately trees that protect and preserve plants and shrubs, bestowing on them life's blessings without ever touching their roots or trunks.

Do not overlook the assets of intercession.

Jesus prayed for his disciples and followers in his final hours.

~ 18 ~

Trials by Fire

And the fire will test what each one's work is. – Paul (1 Cor. 3:13)

The mechanized industry of modern times refers frequently to "trials by fire" for testing the strength of its products, and as we ponder this fact, let us remember that the Gospel also referred to such trials almost twenty centuries ago with respect to spiritual attainments.

In writing to the Corinthians, Paul imagines human workers building upon a single foundation, Jesus Christ, with individuals materializing their own accomplishments in conformity with their evolutionary resources.

Each and every disciple, however, must proceed with their own particular endeavor, fully convinced that times of struggle will expose them to everyone so that their qualities may be correctly evaluated.

The perfecting of the world in its material aspect can furnish an image of the importance of such meaningful evaluations. The earth is replete with riches, positions, standards and minds that cannot withstand trials by fire. The moment they are exposed to purifying processes, they precipitously descend the steps of misery, ruin and decadence. In the service of Christ, it is also just for his followers to expect their own personal capabilities to be tested when the time comes. Character, love, faith, patience and hope represent achievements for the life eternal, accomplished by individuals with the holy assistance of the Master. But all disciples must expect experiences, which, at the right moment, will try their spiritual character.

~ 19 ~

False Accusations

"What have I to do with you, Jesus, Son of God Most High? I beg you not to torment me." – (Lk. 8:28)

The case of the troubled spirit who sensed Jesus' approach and greeted him with desperate questioning presents numerous aspects worthy of study.

The fact that the spirit begged the Divine Master not to torment it demands close attention on the part of sincere disciples.

Who could possibly believe that Christ was capable of inflicting torment on anyone? In this case, it was an ignorant and wicked spirit, who, in its inner madness, was already suffering much because of its own doing. The Master's presence, however, brought it enough clarity to contemplate the suffering of its conscience immersed as it was in the mire of crime and dire rebelliousness. The light chastened its inner darkness, revealing its tortured, compassion-worthy nakedness.

This picture is highly significant for those who dismiss the religious truths of life and view their content as a bitter cup of anguish and suffering. These indifferent and mocking individuals usually say that serving the faith floods the way with tears and clouds the heart.

Such statements, however, betray them. On a greater or lesser scale, these individuals are like the unfortunate brother who accused Jesus Christ of being a minister of torment.

~ 20 ~

The Journey

"Nevertheless, I must walk today, tomorrow and the next day." – Jesus (Lk. 13:33)

It is always important to carry on in the quest for definitive spiritual growth. It is indispensable to press on, overcoming obstacles and darkness, transforming all afflictions and difficulties into steps of ascension.

In outlining his objective, Jesus referred to his journey toward Jerusalem, where his final glorification through martyrdom awaited him. We can apply this same lesson to our own unending experiences, symbolized by our own redemptive testimony's journey toward Jerusalem.

However, we must clarify the characteristics of this journey for the acquisition of eternal values.

Many believe that pressing onward means seeking circumstances of prominence in the world, winning positions of temporary renown or bringing vast financial wealth into one's own personal sphere.

But this is not so.

In this regard, so-called "regular people" perhaps have greater potential for success.

In fleeting situations, the dominant personality's journey is filled with dangers, complex responsibilities and atrocious threats. The feeling of having reached the top increases the feeling of the downfall.

It is imperative to carry on, but the journey is the responsibility of the eternal spirit in the arena of inner acquisitions.

Very often, persons who believe they are at the height of their journey toward the Divine Wisdom are only paralyzed in delusion.

Let no one be fooled by these false rest stops.

It is important to work, to know oneself, to enlighten oneself and to listen to Christ each and every day. In order to imprint this lesson within us, we have been born on the earth to share in its struggles and to spend its bodies, and on it we will be reborn again.

~ 21 ~

Deep Water

And when he had finished speaking, he said to Simon, "Go out into deep water and cast your nets in order to fish." – (Lk. 5:4)

This verse leads us to think about our companions-in-struggle who feel forsaken in the human experience.

A disquieting sensation of loneliness cuts them to the heart.

They weep from longing and pain, renewing their afflictions over and over.

They believe that fate has reserved the cup of unending bitterness for them.

They sorrowfully recall the days of childhood and youth, and the hopes that have been dashed to pieces in the conflicts of the world.

At every moment, they inwardly experience the vague uproar of memories that increase their feelings of emptiness.

The fact is, all mortals experience these periods of anguish.

If someone has not yet experienced them on a particular stretch of the road, their turn will come nevertheless, because, generally speaking, nearly every spirit departs the flesh when the cold signs of winter increase around it.

So, when your time of difficulty arrives, assure yourself that the days for fishing in "deep water" have come to your soul, and that it is time to search for true values without the incentive of certain illusions of the material experience. If you find yourself alone, if you feel forsaken, remember that, beyond the grave, there are friends watching over you and lovingly waiting for you.

The Father never forsakes his children; therefore, if you find yourself without family ties, without true friends on the transitory landscape of the planet, it is because Jesus has sent you into the deep waters of life in order for you to test your acquisitions with hard lessons.

~ 22 ~

Inconstancy

For the one who doubts is like a wave on the ocean, which is lifted by the wind and tossed from place to place. – (Js. 1:6)

Undeniably, there is much scientific and philosophical doubt in the world. Harbored within loyal hearts, such doubt is a precious motivation for acquiring great and uplifting convictions. However, James is referring here to the inconstancy of people who, seeking to receive divine benefits in the form of personal advantages, habitually pursue various courses in the field of intellectual investigation without any intention of trusting in the significant principles of life.

Those who concern themselves with entering through many doors at the same time will end up not entering through any at all.

Frivolousness jeopardizes people in every area of their lives, especially in work positions, in bodily infirmities and in love relationships.

In order for someone to be able to judge a particular experience correctly, they must enumerate the years spent exposed to it, living under its characteristics.

Above all, we must sincerely trust in the Wisdom and Goodness of the Most High, knowing that it is imperative to persevere with a person or a cause that may help us and build us up spiritually.

Inconstant persons are portrayed as the "… wave on the ocean, which is lifted by the wind and tossed from place to place."

When you serve, or when you are waiting for blessings from On High, do not allow yourself to be led by unwholesome anxiety. The Father possesses innumerable means for administering the good, and he is always the same Paternal Lord through all of them. The blessing will reach you, but it depends on you yourself and how you proceed in the constructive struggle, and whether or not you persist in trust, without which the Divine Power will encounter natural obstacles to expressing itself on your pathway.

~ 23 ~

Not Everyone Has It

And pray that we may be delivered from wicked and evil men, for not everyone has faith. – Paul (2 Thes. 3:2)

Addressing his brothers and sisters at Thessalonica, the Apostle to the Gentiles besought their cooperation on behalf of the evangelical endeavor so that the Lord's work could be free of wicked and evil individuals, justifying his appeal with the statement that "not everyone has faith."

Through Paul's words, one can perceive his certainty that evil individuals would infiltrate the centers of Christianizing work, and that their malice could cause harm, making it necessary to mobilize the resources of the spirit against such influences.

In only a few words, the great convert wrote an infinitely valuable warning. In fact, religious color will characterize the outward vestment of entire communities, but faith will be the heritage only of those who work without measuring the sacrifices, for they have brought faith into the sanctuary of their own inner world. The Christian label may be worn by anyone; however, Christian faith will show itself to be pure, unconditional and sublime in very few hearts. Many desire to possess it as if it were a simple bill of exchange, while numerous students of the Gospel invoke it rashly as if it were a wandering butterfly. They forget that if the physical needs of the body demand daily personal effort, the essential needs of the spirit will never be resolved by idle expectancy.

To accept the truth, to seek it and to believe in it are common requirements; however, to maintain a living faith is the divine accomplishment of those who have worked, persisted and suffered to acquire it.

~ 24 ~

Prodigal Children

And when he had come to his senses, he said, "How many of my father's servants have an abundance of bread, while I am here dying of hunger!" – (Lk. 15:17)

In examining the figure of the prodigal son, we all think of him as a rich man who wastes his material wealth on worldly pleasures.

But this picture should be enlarged to entail different aspects.

Prodigal children do not live only where there is an abundance of money. They come from all areas of human activity and wander away from various positions.

Great scientists waste their intelligence by spreading intellectual poisons that are unworthy of the concessions granted to them. Praiseworthy artists needlessly waste their imagination and sensibility on petty adventures, and wind up in debasement and crime.

Everywhere, we see these wasters of wealth, knowledge, time, health and opportunity...

When they see simple and humble people ascending toward God, imbued with real trust, they experience the great anguish of uselessness, and instead of enjoying inner peace, they exclaim downheartedly:

"How many simple laborers hold the bread of inner serenity, whereas the hunger for peace torments my spirit!"

The world is replete with prodigal children, and hour after hour, thousands of voices cry out in despair like this one.

~ 25 ~

On the Path

"And those who are on the path are the ones in whom the word has been sown; but having heard it, Satan soon comes and takes away the word that had been sown in them." – Jesus (Mk. 4:15)

Jesus is our perennial path leading to Divine Love.

Joining him are all the hope-filled spirits of goodwill, sincere adherents of the sanctifying way.

From this blessed and eternal path come the seeds of the Heavenly Light given to ordinary men and women.

It is crucial for people to be aware of this, so that this treasure does not slip by unnoticed.

The sanctifying seed will always appear in the midst of the most varied circumstances.

Just as the generous wind freely spreads the principles of life among the plants, the Invisible Kindness provides all hearts the opportunity of accessing the path of love.

Nearly always, the divine spark appears in ordinary daily activities: in a book, in an insignificant incident at work, or in the timely remark by a friend.

If harmful weeds occupy the soil of your heart, and if you have already received the heavenly principle, cultivate it devotedly, sheltering it in the garden of your soul. The human word may fail, but the Word of the Lord is imperishable. Accept it and comply with it, because if you flee from the imperatives of the eternal life, sooner or later the angel of affliction will visit your spirit, indicating new paths to follow.

~ 26 ~

Immediate Duties

Shepherd God' s flock in your midst, caring for it not because you must, but willingly, according to God's will; not out of greed, but from a ready spirit. – (1 Pet. 5:2)

Of course, if we are able, we should never withhold help or assistance from fellow beings, who, from afar, make a reasonable request for help; however, we must heed Peter's teaching regarding our immediate duties.

There are individuals who willingly give in to disquieting thoughts of disastrous events planned by the sick minds of others, but which probably will never occur. They waste a lot of time prescribing plans of action or uttering pointless lamentations.

To examine other people's lives and future occurrences takes a lot of reflection.

Moreover, it is vital to realize that any difficult problem, either close at hand or farther away, has the purpose of enriching our own lives, enabling us to solve the most intricate enigmas along the way.

That is why Simon Peter's comment is profound and appropriate for all times and situations.

Let us heed the demands of the divine work within our own personal sphere, not out of coercion but out a spontaneous goodwill, leaving our own personal interests behind more and more, and firmly and readily serving the good as much as possible.

At times, it is reasonable to be concerned with the world situation, with the regeneration of communities, or with the positions and responsibilities of others, but we must not overlook "God's flock in our midst."

~ 27 ~

Crushing Evil

And the God of peace will soon crush Satan under your feet. – Paul (Rom. 16:20)

All over the planet, we behold the truceless battle between good and evil.

This great conflict manifests in the most diverse forms. Caught in the vortex of its action, many sensible souls invariably invoke guiding spirits, expecting them to enter the arena and combat the enemies that torment them, defeating them once and for all.

To ask for help or to resort to the law of cooperation is praiseworthy on the part of the spirit who recognizes its own weakness. However, to insist that others take up the efforts that are our own responsibility displays an erroneous assumption that may accentuate our needs.

Satan, representing the power of evil in human life, will be crushed by God; nevertheless, Paul of Tarsus very clearly defines the place of divine victory. The ultimate triumph will occur under human feet.

When, through their own dedication to the work of illumination, people unreservedly entrust themselves to the Father to fulfill his sacrosanct will, forgetting their old animalistic selfishness and comprehending the grandeur of their status as eternal spirits, then they will achieve the sublime victory.

The All-Paternal Lord has already given himself to his terrestrial children, but few are the children who have given themselves to him. Hence, it is crucial not to forget that evil will not be eliminated at random, but rather under the feet of each and every one of us.

~ 28 ~

To What End?

But not all things edify. – Paul (1 Cor. 10:23)

There have always been indefinable individuals who, although they have not done harm to anyone, they have not done any good either.

Examined from the same angle, things along the way must be rightly interpreted in order not to be lost in uselessness.

It is perfectly all right for people to dedicate themselves to literature or to the honest business practices of the world, and no one will contest the laudable character of those who conscientiously choose their individual line of useful work. Nevertheless, it is also right to know the intentions of the writer and the purposes of the business person. What good will it do for the former to produce lengthy works full of verbal fancies and theoretical rapture if his or her words are devoid of constructive thought for the eternal plan of the soul? In what way will the business person profit from his or her immense fortune achieved through hard work and calculation if it remains stagnant in the bank, waiting for the folly of heirs? In either case, one cannot say that either of these individuals had illicit activities in mind; nonetheless, they wasted precious time, forgetting that the smallest things hold a constructive purpose.

Workers who are conscious of their responsibilities do not wander off the righteous path.

There is much affliction and anguish in the workshops of earthly improvement, because the people who work in them are primarily concerned with material gain, overlooking the end for which they are destined. Meanwhile, projects and experiments increase, but the lack of just and necessary spiritual constructiveness continues.

~ 29 ~

The Vineyard

And he said to them, "You too go to the vineyard and I will give you whatever is right." So they went. – (Mt. 20:4)

No one can imagine an earth filled with beauty and potential, but drifting aimlessly in the immensity of the universe.

The planet is not a ship adrift.

Human collectivities customarily fall into disarray, but the laws that preside over the destiny of our earthly home are expressed in complete harmony. This verification helps us understand that the earth is Jesus' vineyard. Here, we can see him working since the dawn of time, and here we can witness the transformation of individuals, who from one experience to the next integrate themselves into his divine love.

The lovely parable of the workers has a profound meaning. In essence, it designates the place of human work, and refers to the many obligations that disciples have received from the

Divine Master.

For the time being, humans hold on to the illusion that the globe can be a stage for racial or political hegemonies. However, over time they will perceive this clamorous error, because all the children of reason who incarnate on the earth bring with them the task of contributing to the achievement of a higher standard of life in the corner in which they are temporarily acting.

Wherever you may be, remember that you are in the Vineyard of Christ.

Are you besieged by difficulty and misfortune?

Even so, work for the common good because the Lord has granted just and suitable material to each and every worker.

~ 30 ~

Formalities

And he said to them, "The Sabbath was made for man; not man for the Sabbath." – (Mk. 2:27)

In this Gospel passage, the Sabbath symbolizes formalities involving human work. In observing these formalities, there are people who sacrifice all possibilities for spiritual progress. Just as there are public service employees who indefinitely put off certain measures that would be beneficial for the whole community because some tiny stamp of approval is missing, there are persons who, because of trifles, forsake great opportunities for uniting with the higher realms.

No one can deny the useful side of formalities. If they were completely useless, the Father would not permit their existence in the scheme of things. They are charts that classify individual efforts and schedules that designate the adequate time for this or that task. However, to make them inflexible precepts or insurmountable obstacles is a grave harm to overall harmony.

Most people heed them more than they obey God himself; however, the Almighty has established all of life's organizations to aid in the evolution and perfecting of all his children.

The planet itself was built for humankind.

If the Creator went to such extremes on behalf of his children, why do we fail in satisfying his divine designs, attaching ourselves to the less important concerns of earthly activity?

Formalities can define, catalog, specify and enumerate, but they should not tyrannize our lives. Remember, they have been put on your path in order to be of assistance to you. Respect them for their constructive and just nature, but do not make them a prison cell.

~ 31 ~

With Charity

"Let all your affairs be done with charity." – Paul (1 Cor. 16:14)

There are still many who do not understand any other sort of charity than the one that dresses humbly on Saturdays and Sundays in order to distribute a little bread to those down on their luck; or a charity that waits for a public calamity to happen before it manifests itself; or one that publishes moving appeals in printed materials.

We cannot question the praiseworthy intentions of this or that group; however, we must realize that the sublime gift of charity is sublime in its reach.

Paul indicates that charity, the kind that expresses Christian love, must embrace all the various activities of our life.

To extend a helping hand and to distribute consolation is to begin the practice of this sublime virtue. All the potentialities of the spirit, however, must eventually be aligned with the divine precept of charity because there is charity in speaking and in listening, in preventing and in allowing, in forgetting and in remembering. A time will come when the mouth, the ears and the feet will be allies of fraternal hands in serving the supreme good.

Each person, like each thing, needs the contribution of goodness in some particular way. Those who lead or those who obey need its holy cooperation in order to be enlightened in the sector they occupy in God's House. Without sublimated love, there will always be darkness, which creates complications.

From now on, carry out your smallest tasks with charity. Even though you may not find direct spiritual recompense in the realm of understanding, you can be sure that the Father devotedly follows all of his children.

Are there rocks and thorns? Set your thoughts on Jesus and press on.

~ 32 ~

Carcasses

"For wherever the carcass is, there the vultures will gather." – (Mt. 24:28)

In presenting the image of the carcass and vultures, the Master was referring to the needs of penitent individuals, who require formidable resources in order to eliminate the darkness in which they are immersed.

A swamp is not dried up by showering it with flowers.

The rotting carcasses out in the field attract vultures that devour them.

This analogy, with its highly symbolic meaning, is one of our Lord's strongest appeals to servants of the Gospel to get involved in sanctifying work.

In various circles of resurgent Christianity, there are those who complain, who are discouraged about the actions of persecutors, obsessors, and visible and invisible tormenters. Some students say that they are under their influence and are thus incapable of following Jesus' designs.

However, much thought should be given before making assertions of this sort, which in reality only accuse those who make them.

One must always remember that merciless birds will gather around abandoned carcasses.

Vultures will seek out other places when the field in which they had been staying is cleaned up.

Individuals who invariably say they are unhappy create the impression that they are living inside a tomb; however, when they make an effort to renew their path, the dark birds of sadness will fly far away.

Fight against the carcasses of any nature that find lodging inside your inner world. Let the divine sun of spirituality enter because as long as you remain a coffin of dead things, you will be hotly pursued by the vultures of destruction.

~ 33 ~

Let Us Work Also

And he said, "People, why are you doing these things? We too are men like you, subject to the same passions." – (Acts 14:15)

The cry of Paul and Barnabas resounds to this day amongst faithful disciples.

The Christian family has quite often desired to perpetuate the illusion of the inhabitants of Lystra.

The missionaries of the Revelation possess no privileges in connection with the personal testimony of their service. The achievements that we would like to point to as a result of grace or some special prerogative are nothing more than these missionaries' profound efforts at learning and applying the teachings of Jesus.

Christ did not use his doctrine to found a system of gods and devotees separated from one another; he created a powerful organism of spiritual transformation for the supreme good, which was meant for all hearts thirsting for light, love and truth.

In the Gospel, we see Magdalene immersed in grievous error; Paul persecuting the ideals of salvation; Peter denying his Divine Friend; Mark battling his own hesitations. But it is also in the Gospel that we see the daughter of Magdala renewed on the redemptive path; the great persecutor converted into a messenger of the Good Tidings; the fragile disciple led towards spiritual glory, and the vacillating collaborator transformed into an evangelist for the entire human race.

Christianity is the blessed fount of the soul's restoration to God.

The error of many followers stems from the idolatry they bestow upon valiant exponents of the living faith, who see in sacrifice the true formula of salvation; they picture them on imaginary thrones and bow at their feet, feeling confused, inept and miserable, forgetting that the Father grants all his children the strength necessary for victory.

Of course, we should all love and respect the great figures of the Christian way; on the other hand, we cannot forget that Paul and Peter, like so many others, left their human weaknesses behind for the heavenly gifts and that, whenever we seek to understand its great mission, Planet Earth is a school of illumination, power and triumph.

~ 34 ~

A Solitary Place

And he said to them, "Come with me to a solitary place and rest a little." – (Mk. 6:31)

Jesus' exhortation to his companions is of singular importance for disciples of the Gospel in all ages.

It is crucial to learn the way of the "solitary place", wherein the Master awaits his followers for constructive rest in his love.

In this invaluable symbol, the inner sanctuary of the heart is thirsting for the divine light.

The Lord was in no way referring only to the solitude of places conducive to meditation, where we can always find living suggestions of a human nature. Instead, he was referring to the silent chamber situated within us.

Furthermore, we cannot forget that the moment it immerses itself in the currents of a higher idealism, the spirit thirsting for divine union finds itself maladjusted and profoundly alone in the world, in spite of serving it daily in conformance with the infallible designs of the Most High.

In the secret temple of the soul, the Christ awaits us in order to replenish our exhausted energies.

People first began to search for that "solitary place" by retreating to monasteries or barren areas; however, the teaching of the Savior has nothing to do with the external world.

Prepare yourself to serve the Divine Kingdom in the city or field in any season, but do not seek rest thoughtlessly, knowing that, quite often, an idle body is torture for the soul. Before anything else, seek to discover that "solitary place" within you, where you will find rest in the company of the Master.

~ 35 ~

The Working Christ

For he who worked effectually in Peter for the apostleship of the circumcision has worked in me for Gentiles. – Paul (Gal. 2:8)

Human vanity has always intended to keep the Christ within the circles of religious sectarianism; Jesus, however, continues his activities wherever the principle of the good flourishes.

Along all the avenues of earthly evolution, we see places of worship attended by troubled outsiders, false believers and unhappy fanatics who light the fires of opinion and keep them burning. Among them, however, are persons of the living faith, who have become sacred vessels of the working Christ.

Simon Peter centralized all the tasks of the newborn Gospel, thereby realigning the aspirations of the chosen people.

Paul of Tarsus was a powerful magnet for the renewal of the Gentiles.

Through both, the same Master expressed himself with a sole objective: the perfecting of human beings for the Divine Kingdom.

It is time to recognize the light of these eternal truths.

Jesus continues to work, and his infinite goodness is revealed in every sector where love is established as the supreme ideal.

Let no one be caught up in unjust complaining, thinking that sincere and devoted disciples are holders of divine privileges. Let each follower make an effort to establish within his or her heart an atmosphere propitious for the manifestations of the Lord and his emissaries. Work, study, serve and help always as you seek out the higher spheres, and you will feel Christ working at your side in your everyday relations.

~ 36 ~

To the End

"But the one who perseveres to the end will be saved." – Jesus (Mt. 24:13)

Here, Jesus is not referring to an end that symbolizes termination, but a purpose, an aim, an objective.

The Gospel will be preached to peoples so that they may understand and achieve the higher goals of life.

It is for this reason that only incarnate spirits who are able to persevere can break out of the chrysalis of the animalistic condition.

When the Master applauded persistence, he was referring to the arduous task of those striving for excellence on the spiritual path.

It is necessary to eliminate false notions of unearned favors from the Divinity.

No one will be able to avoid with impunity the amount of effort required in the endeavor for self improvement.

The doors of heaven are wide open. They have never been closed. However, in order for people to rise to such a height, they need wings of love and wisdom. For this purpose, the Supreme Lord grants an abundance of merciful material to all his children and confers on each one the duty of molding it. Such a task, however, requires tremendous effort. In order to conclude it, days and lifetimes are required. Many lose heart and prefer to remain at a standstill for centuries on end in the labyrinths of the lower spheres; nevertheless, good workers know how to persevere until they reach the divine objectives of the earthly path as they continue on a sublime trajectory towards perfection.

~ 37 ~

It Would Be Useless

He answered, "I have told you already and you did not listen; why do you want to hear it again?" – (Jn. 9:27)

Quite frequently, many religious individuals are concerned about getting their friends to change and they try to impose their own personal convictions on them. They employ long and tiresome discussions with unending verbiage, without accomplishing anything beneficial or constructive.

The sincere heart reborn in faith, however, never proceeds in this manner.

It is crucial to dilute the eagerness of superiority that infests the sentiments of many of today's disciples once they are led to new stages of knowledge in the gradated revelation of the divine wisdom, for arguers with evil inclinations take it upon themselves to hinder their progress.

The reply of the man blind from birth to the shrewd and inquiring Jews represents an effective standard for sincere disciples.

Of course, Jesus' followers will not hesitate to offer an explanation regarding the Master, but if they have already done so and have tried to benefit their brother or sister with the values that they believe in, without successfully gaining his or her understanding, why pursue it further? If someone has heard the truth but has not understood it, he or she displays obvious signs of spiritual paralysis. So, it would be useless for him or her to continue to listen over and over, because no one can deceive time. The learned individual who persisted in challenging the unlearned one would be very foolish.

Therefore, do not waste your time on detailed and repetitive explanations to someone who is incapable of understanding them before he or she is overtaken by the sun, the rain, the fire and the water of experience.

You have a thousand resources for working on behalf of your friend, without imposing your way of being and your faith on him or her.

~ 38 ~

Your Personal Account

"Ah! If you only knew today what would bring you peace!" – Jesus (Lk. 19:42)

Jesus' remark as he approached Jerusalem applies much more to the human heart – the living temple of the Lord – than to the physical city, destined to ruin and disintegration in the realms of human experience.

Let us imagine what the world would be like if every person knew what relates to their inner peace.

Due to the almost universal lack of attention to this imperative of life, men and women get caught up in dolorous conflicts, thus acquiring bitter debts.

Let us heed the Master's statement, "If only you knew today..."

These words invite us to ponder our current availability to serve and to reflect on the time we have wasted. They compel us to meditate on the work opportunities that are always available for industrious spirits.

Incarnate individuals have a glorious time temporarily available to them and which has been provided by the Almighty for their personal renewal.

It is important for each one of us to recognize what we need for our own peace of mind. If each individual would maintain a worthy attitude of comprehension of his or her own personal obligations, the ghosts of disquiet would be kept at bay. If everyone were mindful of their particular duties, two thirds of the world's social problems would be resolved naturally.

Pay attention to the minor needs of your immediate circle and answer to them for your own benefit.

You will not walk amongst the stars until you have trod the humble path ahead of you.

~ 39 ~

Invitation to the Good

"But when you are invited, go..." – Jesus (Lk. 14:10)

In all ages, the good is the divine fount capable of providing us with immortal values.

Mindful individuals will have noticed that the entire period of childhood consists of a string of appeals to the sublime fountainhead.

The sacred invitation is repeated year after year. It comes to us by way of our loving parents, our academic mentors, wholesome reading material, religious sentiments and ordinary friends.

However, few minds reach adolescence with their attention set on a lofty calling. Most people listen to the demands of their lower nature and neglect their precious obligations.

The appeals persist nonetheless...

Here, it might be a friendly book silently revealing the truth; there, it might be a generous friend who insists on pointing out the importance of the enlightening realities of life...

Rebellious persons, however, even during full adulthood, usually laugh unconscientiously at any such appeals. Nevertheless, whether they like it or not, they are heading for natural disenchantments that impose more-balanced thoughts.

In Jesus' Gospel, the invitation to the good is clothed in eternal clarity. By heeding it, we can proceed towards an uninterrupted encounter with our Father.

If the Christian trumpet has reached your ears, accept its appeal without wavering.

Do not wait for the pinprick of necessity.

During the storm, it becomes ever more difficult to see the port.

The majority of our brothers and sisters on earth make their way towards God under the compunction of pain; therefore, do not wait for the lashing of the darkness when you can calmly follow the clear paths of love.

~ 40 ~

In Preparation

"The Lord says: 'I will put my laws in their mind and I will write them on their heart. I will be their God and they will be my people.'" – Paul (Heb. 8:10)

We will translate the Gospel
Into all languages,
For all cultures,
Exalting its magnificence,
Emphasizing its sublimity,
Sowing its poetry,
Commenting on its truth,
Interpreting its lessons,
Impressing it on our reasoning,
Perfecting our hearts...
And reforming our minds,
Renewing laws,

Improving customs,
And lighting pathways…
But the time will come
When the Glad Tidings will need to be engraved within us
In the folds of our minds,
In the recesses of our hearts,
Through words and actions,
Principles and ideals,
Aspirations and hopes,
Gestures and thoughts.
Because, truthfully,
If heaven enables us to spread its Divine Message to the world,
One day, it will ask us to convert ourselves
Into living translations of the Gospel on earth.

~ 41 ~

In the Future

"No longer will anyone teach his neighbor, or each one his brother, saying, 'Know the Lord,' for all will know me, from the least to the greatest." – Paul (Heb. 8:11)

When men and women finally engrave on their souls
The luminous passages of the Divine Law,
Friend will not reproach friend;
Sibling will not denounce sibling.
Prisons will close their doors;
Courts will fall silent.
Cannons will be turned into ploughs;
Armed soldiers will go back to tilling the soil.
Hatred will be expelled from the world;
Bayonets will be put to rest.
Machines will not hurl flames of fire and death,
But will peacefully care for the progress of the planet.

Justice will be surpassed by love.
Children of faith will not only be just
But good, profoundly good.
Prayer will be composed of happiness and praise,
And houses of worship will be consecrated to the sublime task of supreme fraternity.
The preaching of the Law
Will live in the deeds and thoughts of all
Because the Lamb of God
Will have transformed the hearts of all humankind
Into tabernacles of eternal light,
Wherein His Divine Kingdom
Will shine forever.

~ 42 ~

Forever Alive

"God is not the God of the dead, but of the living. Therefore, you err greatly." – Jesus (Mk. 12:27)

In following established conventions in our dealings with our incarnate friends, from time to time we refer to the spirit life by utilizing the word "death" in this or that sentence of normal conversation. However, it is imperative to view death not as the cessation of life but its active transformer.

Spiritually speaking, we are only familiar with a fearsome type of death: that of our consciousness darkened by evil, tortured by remorse or paralyzed on the precipices that border the path of irrationality and crime.

The time has come for us to realize that we are all alive in the Eternal Creation.

Because this knowledge is not yet fully grasped by humankind, great errors occur. The Roman Catholic Church created an artificial heaven and hell in its theology; many Evangelical Protestant groups hold to the literal belief that the physical body – the material clothing of the spirit – will some day rise from the grave in violation of the principles of nature; numerous Spiritists view us spirits as vague and ethereal laboratory phantoms or flickering forms, roaming around with nowhere to go.

Whosoever passes through the grave goes on working, and here, as well as there on the earth, there is disorder only for the disorderly. On the earth's surface or beyond its limits, we invariably continue to live.

So, do not forget that discarnates are neither magicians nor fortunetellers. They are simply brothers and sisters who continue to struggle to improve. We encounter death only on the paths of evil, where darkness impedes the glorious vision of life.

Let us heed the lesson of the Gospel and never forget that our Father is the God of living immortals.

~ 43 ~

Good Manners

"... and sit in the lowest place..." – Jesus (Lk. 14:10)

In this passage, the Master provides an unforgettable lesson in good manners.

The phrase obviously reveals a highly symbolic content that alludes to the paternal banquet of Divine Goodness; however, it would be appropriate to extend the concept in order to apply it to the mechanisms of everyday life.

The Savior's recommendation applies to all situations in which we are called to participate as newcomers among our fellow humans; for instance, entering a home or participating in a meeting for the first time. A person who comes across as a know-it-all or as someone who is superior to everyone else becomes intolerable to those present.

Even if it is the case of a group misguided in its goals or intentions, it would be unreasonable for knowledgeable individuals attending for the very first time to turn themselves into stern and demanding lecturers. For the task of rectifying or guiding souls, faithful workers of the good must make an effort to reach out to these hearts through the ties of genuine fraternity. Only in this way will they effectively eliminate imperfections, each day eradicating a bit of darkness through constant service.

We know that Jesus was the great reformer of the world; however, correcting and spreading love, he affirmed that he had come to humankind to fulfill the Law.

Do not hog the spotlight wherever you go. And whenever you are with your brothers and sisters, do not overshadow them with a display of how much you have accomplished in the realms of love and wisdom. If you have decided to cooperate for the good of others, dim yourself somehow so that others can truly understand you. By imposing rules or exhibiting power, you will be doing nothing but causing trouble.

~ 44 ~

Healing

"Heal the sick and say to them, 'The Kingdom of God has come to you.'" – Jesus (Lk. 10:9)

Of course, Jesus healed many sick people and entrusted them to his disciples in a very special way. However, the Heavenly Physician did not forget to call to the Divine Kingdom those who held on to their human imperfections.

We are not interested only in regenerating the vessel through which we express ourselves, but above all, in correcting the spirit.

May humankind be freed from illnesses, but it must also understand the value of health. It is indeed as difficult for us to understand the hidden lesson of diseases in the body as it is to assimilate the call to sanctifying work that beckons to us through our physical healthiness.

Would the Lord allow cellular harmony just so a corrupt will could strike it and injure it to the detriment of the spirit?

Infirm persons desire the readjustment of their vital energies; however, they must learn prudence and value the elements that have been placed at their disposal in the constructive earthly experience.

There are sick individuals who complain about being bedridden and weep in their affliction, not because they want to renew their concepts regarding the sacred principles of life, but because they are unable to continue their reckless behavior.

It is always useful to heal the sick when there is permission from a higher order to do so, but in light of such a gift from the Most High, individuals interested in this blessing should reconsider the issues that concern them and realize that a new day has dawned on their spirit on the redemptive path.

~ 45 ~

When You Pray

"And while you are praying, forgive." – Jesus (Mk. 11:25)

The sincere attitude of a soul at prayer does not obey ordinary mechanical movements. While involved in the daily struggle, people invariably heed the automatisms of the material aspect of life, which changes unnoticeably over time; however, when the soul turns toward the divine sanctuaries of the higher planes through prayer, one's consciousness is put in contact with the eternal and creative meaning of the infinite life.

All disciples should examine the sensations they experience when they pray to the Most High and understand that it is crucial for them to maintain their inner peace before people and circumstantial conditions on the pathway.

A mind that prays is active in the invisible realms.

Even when they do not know each other in the arena of conventional activities, incarnate minds communicate with one another through the delicate fibers of the wishes manifested in prayer. In such instances, which we should consecrate exclusively to the highest part of our individuality, we send out messages, appeals, intentions, plans and concerns that seek a suitable objective.

Those who consciously or unconsciously utilize this opportunity to expand the currents of evil are to be pitied. That is why Jesus, being aware of how rare guilt-free men and women are, offered this expressive plan of love to the benefit of every disciple of the Gospel: "And while you are praying, forgive."

~ 46 ~

You, However

But we who are strong ought to bear the failings of the weak and not just please ourselves. – Paul (Rom. 15:1)

For what purpose do human beings acquire the righteous notion of faith in God? To evade the struggle and live their lives waiting to go to heaven?

Such an attitude would be incomprehensible.

Disciples gain the light of understanding in order to put it into practice on their own pathway. Jesus has granted them a piece of heaven for them to develop it and extend it across the land on which they walk.

To receive sacred assistance from the Master only to avoid the workshop of redemption is to display extreme ignorance.

To give oneself to Christ means working to establish his kingdom.

Since they lack an understanding of the truth, earth's places of worship are replete with paralyzed souls who have deserted their own efforts in their yearning for heavenly bliss. This can be understood in individuals who have not yet acquired the necessary sense of reality. But you, who are more versed in knowledge, should not rest in indifference before the sacred duties of the light that shines in your inner world through the infinite goodness of the Christ. It is imperative for everybody to take up their work tools in the task they are responsible for, striving for the victory of the good in the circle of persons and activities that surround them.

Many sick spirits, overtaken by false preoccupations and worldly idleness, can plead ignorance. You, however, are not weaklings, nor are you lacking in the Lord's mercy.

47

The Difficulty of Pleasing Others

"If I were still pleasing men, I would not be a servant of Christ." – Paul (Gal. 1:10)

Sincere disciples of the Gospel should concern themselves with their own endeavors and with the isolated and peaceful approval of their conscience in the tasks they are called to perform each day, learning to do without the unreasonable opinions of the world.

The masses do not know how to display warmth and admiration except toward those who meet their demands and whims. In the conflicts characteristic of their spiritual progress, faithful disciples of Jesus will be a different type of worker that the masses, in their instinctive impulses, will not be able to understand.

Messengers of the Glad Tidings who show concern about how the world regards them will reveal much inexperience and lack of watchfulness. When they find themselves in material prosperity, in which the Master grants them more precise comfort, neighbors will maliciously inquire as to the cause of their consecutive successes. On the other hand, when they encounter poverty and difficulties, people will attribute these problematic experiences to supposed defections from the sublime ideals they have espoused.

It is indispensable to labor on behalf of others as someone who is aware that the whole work belongs to Jesus Christ. The world will eventually understand the great efforts of sincere servants, but perhaps at another time, when its evolutionary ascension enables it to.

On many occasions, popular opinions are a noisy group of children who cannot stand highly inspired teachers on the subject of order and progress, work and achievement.

Therefore, may sincere workers for Christ strive without being concerned with the faulty judgments of others. Jesus knows the good worker, and that is enough.

48

Let Us Understand

"You did not desire sacrifices and offerings, burnt offerings and sin offerings, nor did they please you." – Paul (Heb. 10:8)

The people of the ancient world did not understand their relation to the Most High except through magnificent offerings and burnt sacrifices.

Certain primitive peoples reached exceptional religious extravagance, bringing human blood to their altars.

Such regrettable manifestations dwindled down throughout the centuries; however, even today, lamentable outbreaks of eccentricity still occur in offerings of this nature.

Christianity brought about a complete renewal in the understanding of the divine truths; however, even among its ranks absurd promises still surface, which only promote the introduction of ignorance and vice.

The greatest notion of God to be harbored in the sanctuary of our spirit has been presented to us by Jesus, who revealed God as a loving and just Father awaiting our testimonies of understanding and love.

On the earth itself, any conscientious and honest head of the family does not wish for his or her children to make useless offerings for the purpose of softening his or her affectionate watch-care. If such initiatives are not agreeable to capricious and fallible human parents, how could we possibly attribute such fault to the All Merciful for the purpose of winning heavenly merit?

It is indispensable to strive to change this dire misinterpretation.

Genuine happiness is only possible in the Christian home when its members fulfill the obligations assigned to them, even under the weight of heroic decisions. The case is no different with our Heavenly Father, because the Supreme Lord does not request sacrifices and tears, but serene disposition to accept his sublime will, putting it into practice.

~ 49 ~

An Old Argument

"And upon offering this in his [Paul's] defense, Festus exclaimed loudly, 'You are crazy, Paul! Your great learning is making you delirious.'" (Acts 26:24)

It is very common to launch against the disciples of the Gospel the false accusation of madness, ascribed to them by this century's proponents of scientism.

This is an age-old argument on the part of those who, complacent in their errors, want to flee the truth.

There are workers who waste valuable time, lamenting that the crowds classify them as mentally unbalanced. This is no reason for barren arguments.

On many occasions, the Master himself was assumed to be demented, and the apostles received no other designation.

In one of his final arguments we see Paul, the valiant friend of the gentiles, facing the Provincial Court of Caesarea, proclaiming the immortal truths of Jesus Christ. The assembly is overcome with amazement. Paul's noble and sincere speech petrifies the audience. It is at this time that Portius Festus, as the leader of the guests, decides to break down the vibration of fear that dominates the environment. But before doing so, however, this astute Roman realized that he first had to justify his actions on a sound basis. But how could he accuse the great convert of Damascus if he, Festus, was aware of Paul's honest character, his sincere humility, his sublime patience and his burning spirit of sacrifice? He then remembers Paul's "great learning," and he calls him crazy because of the divine knowledge to which he bore witness.

So remember this self-denying warrior and do not be affected by false references from those who try to provoke you into abandoning the truth. Evil is incompatible with the good, and with "little learning" or with "great learning," from the moment you enroll as a member of the disciples of Jesus, the inferior world will not be short of its sarcasm and persecution.

~ 50 ~

Save Yourself

"Go, and sin no more." – Jesus (Jn. 8:11)

The precious seed that you do not care for can be lost.

The young tree that you fail to protect is open to destruction.

The spring that you do not look after could dry up.

The water that you fail to release may become a swamp.

The fruit that you do not eat becomes spoiled.

The good earth that you fail to till becomes asphyxiated by useless weeds.

The hoe that you do not use becomes rusty.

The flowers that you fail to cultivate do not always rebloom.

The friend you do not keep avoids your path.

The medication whose proper dosage you do not abide by will not benefit you physically.

The same applies to Divine Grace.

If you do not guard the blessings from On High, respecting them within you; if you do not utilize the elevated knowledge that you have received for the benefit of your own happiness; if you do not appreciate the contribution that has come down to you from above, then the dedication of spirit messengers is of no value to you. In vain will they perform miracles of love and patience in solving your problems, because without the cooperation of your will in the regenerative process, all their saving measures will be futile.

"Go and sin no more."

Jesus' teaching is expressive and sufficient.

The Divine Physician provides the cure, but if we do not keep it within us, no one can foresee the extent and consequences of the new imbalances that will besiege our lack of vigilance.

~ 51 ~

Help Yourself

"...preaching the Gospel of the Kingdom and healing all infirmities." (Matt. 9:35)

Heal your cataracts and your conjunctivitis, but correct your eyes' spiritual sight also.

Protect yourself against deafness, but correct your way of registering the voices and various requests directed to you.

Take medication for your arrhythmia and dyspnea, but do not hand your heart over to ruinous impulsivity.

Fight against neurasthenia and exhaustion, but focus on readjusting your emotions and tendencies.

Treat your gastric disorder, but tame your appetite at the dinner table.

Improve your blood's condition, but do not overburden it with the residues of inferior pleasures.

Combat hepatitis, but free your liver from the excesses you surrender to.

Remove the dangers of uremia, but do not suffocate your kidneys with the poisons in shiny goblets.

Dislodge the rheumatism from your limbs, but also pay attention to what you do with your feet, arms and hands.

Heal the brain dysfunctions that threaten you, but learn to keep your mind on higher idealism and noble acts.

Consecrate yourself to your own personal healing, but do not forget to preach the Divine Kingdom to *your physical organs*. They are alive and can be educated. Without purifying your thoughts and without your will commanding the ship of your organism toward the good, the intervention of human remedies will be no more than a transitory measure for uselessness.

~ 52 ~

Subtle Dangers

"Therefore, do not make yourselves into idolaters." – Paul (1 Cor. 10:7)

Paul's recommendation to the Corinthians should be remembered and applied at all times in the endeavors of ascension pursued by the world's religions.

It is imperative to avoid idolatry in all circumstances. Its manifestations have always represented serious dangers for the spiritual life.

The ancient beliefs are still replete with outward forms of worship and dead idols.

The Consoler, sent to the world in the venerable Spiritist mission, will always be on the lookout for this poisonous process of soul paralysis.

Here and there appear forms of worship that must be fought against. They are no longer images from human circles or physical instruments supposedly sanctified for use in conventional ceremonies, but friendly spirits and incarnate mediums that are unconsciously and inadvertently enthroned on the frail altar of illusory honors. It is necessary to recognize that therein lies a subtle danger, through which innumerable disciples have slid into the precipice of uselessness.

Inopportune praise usually deludes dedicated but inexperienced mediums, in addition to creating a certain environment of misunderstanding that impedes the spontaneous manifestation of true friends of righteousness from the spirit plane.

No one should overlook the condition of relative purification of the discarnate messengers who communicate and the immediate necessities of life of human mediums.

Let us combat the false idols that threaten Christian Spiritism. Let each disciple utilize the ample resources of the law of cooperation, focusing on his or her own personal efforts with sincere devotion to the task, and let us all remember that in the apostolate of the Divine Master, love and fidelity to God constituted the central theme.

~ 53 ~

In Chains

"For which I am an ambassador in chains so that I may speak of him freely, as I should." – Paul (Eph. 6:20)

In this passage we observe the apostle to the gentiles making a statement that appears contradictory at first glance.

Paul states that his condition is that of an emissary in chains, while at the same time declaring that it has happened so that he can serve the Gospel as freely as needed.

The great worker was addressing the followers at Ephesus, referring to his distressing situation as a prisoner of the Roman authorities; nevertheless, because of this and in light of his difficult testimony, his spirit was freer for the service that he had to render.

This image is significant for those who wish for economic and financial independence, or for greater freedom in the world in order to exemplify the teachings of the gospel. There are many people who say that they are waiting for days of material abundance and earthly advantages in order to attend to Christian ideals. This, however, is nonsensical. Serving Jesus can happen everywhere.

Paul, in chains, felt freer to preach the Truth. Of course, not all disciples will have to experience such high peaks of testimony. But all, without distinction, bring along with them the saintly chains of their daily obligations in the home, at work, in their hourly routines, in the midst of society and in the family.

None, therefore, should try to break their chains, erroneously believing that they will be a candidate for a better position in the workshop of the Christ.

Only our duties correctly fulfilled will confer us access to real freedom.

54

The Reason for Evocations

"When I was called, I came without arguing. So I would ask: why did you send for me?" – Peter (Acts 10:29)

The question that Peter asked the Centurion Cornelius is of great significance in the Acts of the Apostles.

This Roman officer had the reputation of being an upright and charitable man. He solicited the presence of the disciple of Jesus to attend to matters of a higher moral order after receiving generous counsel from an emissary from Heaven. However, upon arriving at Cornelius' home, the levelheaded former fisherman from Capernaum asked:

"Why did you send for me?"

Simon needed to know the reason for this request just as conscientous workers would like to know exactly where they stand and why they have been summoned to someone else's field.

This expressive picture proposes many considerations to new students of the Gospel.

Many people, upon hearing references made to this or that high order spirit, would like to invoke its presence in doctrinal meetings.

Such a decision, however, would be both untimely and senseless.

Why request company we do not deserve?

We do not have to attribute this impulse to frivolity, but we must try to evaluate the importance of the purposes at play.

Let us imagine summoning Simon Peter to a particular prayer meeting, and let us suppose that the venerable apostle acquiesces. Naturally, you would be obliged to explain to this great heavenly emissary the reason for your request. And basing our mental attitudes on good sense, let us ask ourselves if we are spiritually mature enough to see, to listen and to understand this glorious spirit. Which one of us would respond affirmatively? Would we have the audacity to invoke the sublime Cephas merely to hear him speak?

~ 55 ~

Invisible Qualities

"For since the creation of the world, his invisible qualities, as well as his eternal power and divinity, have been understood and clearly seen through the things that were created." – Paul (Rom. 1:20)

The spectacle of the Creation of the Universe is the strongest of all manifestations against negativistic materialism, the child of ignorance or folly.

The created things are the ones that speak most correctly about the invisible nature.

Where is the activity that unfolds without a base?

Every intelligent form has been born from an intelligent source.

People only know the causes of their transitory achievements, ignoring, however, the complex reasons for each angle along the way. The outer landscape that affects the senses is a minuscule part of the heritage of divine creations that sustain their habitat, which is conditioned to their ability to utilize it. Human eyes will not see beyond the limit of what they can bear. Individuals will live among beings they need in their efforts to perfect themselves, and will receive an adequate environment for their improvement and progress. However, let no one limit the vital manifestations of the sphere in which they live by what their mortal fingers are capable of touching.

The objects visible in the realm of ephemeral forms are brief and transitory, resulting from the invisible forces of the eternal plane.

Fulfill your obligations and you will receive the rights that await you. Correctly fulfill what this day asks of you and you will not have to repeat the same experience tomorrow.

~ 56 ~

Successes and Failures

"I know how to live in need and I also know how to live in abundance." – Paul (Phil. 4:12)

In every social community there are numerous individuals overly preoccupied with their particular successes, anxiously awaiting the opportunity for recognition. They are precisely the ones who are least able to maintain distinguished positions when invited to the highest posts in the world, disastrously ruining the opportunities for elevation that life grants them.

Almost always, those who have learned to endure poverty are the ones who know how to manage their material resources more effectively.

For this reason, accumulated treasures in the hands of those who have not worked for it is often the cause of crime, division, and perturbation.

Honest, hard-working parents will form a mentality of personal effort and affective cooperation in their children, whereas selfish and uncaring parents will foster uselessness and laziness in theirs.

Paul of Tarsus, in his message to the Philippian church, refers to the precious imperative on the path relating to equilibrium, demonstrating the need of the disciple as to the value of poverty and wealth, of scarcity and abundance.

Success and failure are two cups filled with diverse elements that may nonetheless be adapted to the same sublime purpose. Human ignorance, however, finds the liquor of exhilaration in the first, and the bile of desperation in the second. Therein lies a profound mistake, because the wise person will extract the divine content from happiness and pain, abundance or scarcity.

~ 57 ~

In Jesus' Presence

"And whatever you do, do it with all your heart, as for the Lord and not for men." – Paul (Col. 3:25)

Among human beings, the understanding of the work of Christ will in the future reach the required scope for the glorification of the One who has watched over us closely from the very first day, illuminating our path with the Divine Light.

If learned persons would ask themselves what the essential reason for their activities on earth is, they would always find in their inner sanctuary vast horizons for conclusions of infinite value.

For whom have they been working all this time?

To whom have they offered the fruit of their daily work?

We do not wish to demean the respectable position of countries, organizations, family, or the individual; however, we cannot fail to recognize their position of relativity in time. As the years roll on, borders change, laws evolve, the household group is renewed and humankind progresses toward higher and higher destinies.

Everything that represents personal effort has been accomplished through individuals' own initiative in the field of Christ's permanent work. Whatever we have accomplished through the centuries constitutes either a benefit or an offense to ourselves in the work that belongs to the Lord and not to us. Law makers and governed people pass through time with the baggage that is their own, and Jesus remains in order to evaluate the advantage or disadvantage of the cooperation of each one of them in the divine service of evolution and improvement.

Administration and obedience, the responsibility of leading and following, are only subdivisions of the stewardship conferred by the Lord on his wards.

Dignified work is a holy opportunity. Within the circles of service, the attitude assumed by men and women will either honor or dishonor their immortal personality in the presence of Jesus Christ.

~ 58 ~

Contributing

"Let each contribute according to what he has decided in his heart; not sadly or out of necessity, for God loves what is given out of joy." – Paul (2 Cor. 9:7)

Paul's statement that God loves what is given out of joy is understood by many as referring only to material charity.

Praise, however, is not restricted to generous hands that distribute small donations of goodness to the needy and to the suffering.

Of course, all gestures of love receive divine recognition, but we must remember that the word "contributing" in the current lesson appears in all its sublimity.

Cooperation in the good is a pulsating matter everyday and everywhere. Any individual is capable of extending it. It is not only the beggar who hopes for it, but also the cradle where all experience is renewed, the family in which we refine our virtuous accomplishments, our neighbor, our brother or sister in humanity, and the workplace, which signals our own individual improvement in our daily efforts.

At the moment of nightly rest, each heart can question itself regarding the quality of its cooperation at work, in conversations, in affectionate relationships, or in this or that everyday life endeavor.

Let us be cautious regarding unproductive sadness and gloom. Ill will, complaints, dissatisfaction, and frivolities are not part of the labor that the Lord expects from our activities in the world. Let us mobilize our resources optimistically, and let us not forget that the Father loves the child that contributes with joy.

59

Let Us Proceed until We Are There

"If you remain in me and my words remain in you, ask whatever you wish, and it will be done for you." – Jesus (Jn. 15:7)

In the Lord's Prayer, Jesus explains to his followers the need for full adherence to the Father's designs.

The Master knew that the human will is still quite fragile and that numerous struggles surround the individual until he or she learns to establish unity with the Divine.

In spite of this, the lesson of that prayer has been interpreted by most believers as an easy recourse for obtaining celestial aid.

Many request special favors and mechanically recite verbal formulas. Of course, they cannot receive the immediate satisfaction of their personal whims, because in the fallen or ignorant state, the spirit needs, more than anything else, to learn to submit to the divine designs.

However, there will come a time when prayers are fully answered. We will accomplish this when we become spiritually in Christ. At that point, whatever we desire will be done because we will have perceived the correct meaning of each thing and the purpose of each circumstance. We will be able to want and to request in Jesus, and life will present itself in its true characteristics of infinity, eternity, renewal and beauty.

Whether incarnate or discarnate, we are still walking toward the Master in order that we may experience glorious union with his love. Until then, let us work and be vigilant in order to understand the divine will.

~ 60 ~

The Logic of Providence

"After you were illumined, you endured a great struggle against afflictions." – Paul (Heb. 10:32)

Usually those who cultivate a sincere faith are considered great sufferers in the world.

In fact, there are those who affirm that they deliberately avoid from religious circles because they fear the contagion of spiritual suffering.

In everyday life, the godless, the ignorant and the frivolous exhibit themselves spectacularly through bizarre shades of outward fantasy. However, as they approach the heavenly truths before attaining access to the lasting joys of a higher spirituality, they pass through long tunnels of sadness, downheartedness, and taciturnity. This is natural, for there will always be much soul searching after insanity and remorse brought on by immoderation.

The problem, however, entails a larger explanation.

The mercy that is manifested in God's justice transcends human comprehension.

The Father confers on his ignorant and lost children the right of more trying experiences only after they have been enlightened. Only after they have learned to see with their eternal spirit will life offer them different values. From that moment on, the strength needed to triumph in the great battle of afflictions will be born in their hearts.

In spite of their appearances, frivolous persons and opportunists are usually frail souls, whose withered branches will break at the first blow of the storm. Noble spirits, who are able to withstand the torments of the earthly pathway, are well aware of this. Only spiritual enlightenment guarantees success in trials.

No one entrusts the responsibility of a ship encumbered with preoccupations and dangers to mere children.

~ 61 ~

Men and Women with Jesus

Rejoice in the Lord always; again, I say rejoice. – Paul (Phil. 4:4)

With Jesus, men and women rise
From the darkness to the light…
From idleness to service…
From ignorance to wisdom…
From instinct to reason…
From might to right…
From selfishness to fraternity …
From tyranny to compassion…
From violence to understanding…
From hatred to love…
From deceitful possession to the search for imperishable assets…

From bloody conquest to edifying self-denial…
From extortion to justice…
From hardness of heart to mercy…
From the empty word to the creative word…
From monstrosity to beauty…
From vice to virtue…
From disharmony to harmony…
From affliction to contentment…
From the swamp to the mountain…
From the quagmire to glory…

My brothers and sisters, let us rejoice fully in the redemptive struggle!

What angelic pinnacles could we not reach if we truly consecrate ourselves to the Divine Friend who descended and humiliated himself for us?

~ 62 ~

Jesus for Men and Women

And being in form as a man, he humbled himself, being obedient to death, the death of a cross. – Paul (Phil. 2:8)

The Master came down in order to serve,
From splendor to darkness...
From eternal dawn to complete night...
From the stars to the manger...
From the infinite to limitation...
From glory to carpentry...
From grandeur to self-denial...
From the divinity of the angels to the misery of humankind...
From the company of sublime spirits to the company of sinners...
From being governor of the world to being servant of all...

From magnanimous creditor to slave...
From benefactor to persecuted...
From savior to one forsaken...
From emissary of love to victim of hatred...
From redeemer of the ages to prisoner of the shadows...
From heavenly shepherd to oppressed lamb...
From a powerful throne to the cross of martyrdom...
From the sanctifying Word to anguished silence...
From advocate for his creatures to defenseless defendant...
From the arms of friends to the company of thieves...
From giver of life eternal to one sentenced to the valley of death...

He humbled himself and dimmed his light so that men and women could rise and shine forever!

O Lord! What have you not done for us so that we might learn the way of Glorious Resurrection into you Kingdom?

63

The Lord always Provides

> *"If you then, being evil, know how to give good gifts to your children, how much more will your Heavenly Father give the Holy Spirit to those who ask Him?"* – Jesus (Lk. 11:13)

In spite of the blind love that often envelops his heart, an earthly father always knows how to surround his child with worthwhile gifts.

Why would the Heavenly Father, full of wisdom and love, remain deaf and unmoved regarding our supplications?

The paternal devotion of the Supreme Lord surrounds us everywhere. It is important, however, for us not to twist our understanding of it.

We must remember that Divine Providence invariably operates for the infinite good.

It frees the asphyxiating atmosphere with the elements of the storm.

It defends the flower with thorns.

It sustains the productive farm with smelly fertilizer.

It protects the green of the valleys with the hardness of the rocks.

It is the same in circles of planetary struggle. Events that seem to be disastrous to our personal activity are actually props for our equilibrium and success, while occurrences we interpret as collective calamities constitute enormous public benefits.

Pray, therefore, to the Lord for the blessing of the Divine Light for your heart and mind so that you do not get lost in the maze of your problems. However, do not forget that on most occasions help from heaven first comes to us via ordinary avenues, through anguish and disappointment. Nevertheless, wait trustingly for the passage of time, for time silently explains everything and will reveal to your heart the infinite kindness of the Father, who restores the health of our soul through the thorns of disillusionment or the bitter cup of suffering.

~ 64 ~

Better to Suffer Doing Good

For it is better that you suffer doing good (if it is God's will) than doing evil. (1 Pet. 3:17)

In order to amass financial resources, which they will have to suddenly leave behind, people often catch deplorable illnesses that corrode their energy centers, causing unwelcome death.

By purchasing ephemeral pleasures for their body of flesh, they commonly reap dangerous infirmities that accompany them till the end of the days of the physical vessel in which they move about on earth.

By getting angry over insignificant lessons along the way, they poison their vital organs, thereby creating fatal imbalances for their physical life.

By stuffing their stomachs on certain occasions, they corrupt important components of their physiological instrumentality, renouncing the perfection of their corporeal vessel for the mere pleasure of gluttony.

Why dread the difficulties of the well-lit path of love and wisdom when the dark trail of hatred and ignorance is replete with vengeful and disturbing forces?

How can we fear fatigue and exhaustion, complications and misunderstandings, conflicts and disappointments arising from the blessed struggle for the supreme victory of the good when the fight for the temporary triumph of evil leads combatants to the spoils of affliction and suffering?

Let us utilize our highest potential in service to Christ, pledging our lives to him.

The criminal weapon and the repugnant act perpetrated by it provoke cursing and darkness, but for workers wounded while performing their duty, and for the lamp that goes out while giving off its light, a different destiny is reserved.

~ 65 ~

Let Us Be at Peace

Live in peace with one another. – Paul (1 Thess. 5:13)

If it is impossible to live in a climate of perfect peace due to the ignorance and hostility that dominate the human pathway, it is logical for disciples to seek inner serenity when faced with the conflicts that seek to envelop them at every moment.

Each incarnate mind is an extensive center of spiritual government, subordinate for the time being to appropriate limitations while served by various abilities expressed in the senses and perceptions.

Once all the individual power centers become self-controlled and are geared toward the real good, then wars will be banished from the planet.

To achieve this, however, those of humankind's brothers and sisters who are older in experience and knowledge must learn to live in peace with one another.

Educating the sight, hearing, taste and impulses represents the primordial foundation for constructive peacefulness.

We usually hear, see and feel according to our inclinations and not according to what is real. We interpret certain pieces of information according to our inner disharmony rather than the good intentions in which they were initially sent. We observe situations and events with the light or darkness that infuses our mind. We feel with the reflection or chaos we have instilled in our own understanding.

For this reason, serenity must envelop our steps as much as possible as we face the conflicts that surround us in our present circumstance.

Without calmness, it is impossible to discern and to work for the good.

Without peace inside of us, we will never reach the realms of true peace.

66

Good Will

See to it that you live prudently. – Paul (Eph. 5:15)

Good will finds work to be done.
Work leads to renewal.
Renewal finds the good.
The good expresses the spirit of service.
The spirit of service brings understanding.
Understanding brings humility.
Humility wins love.
Love leads to self-denial.
Self-denial reaches the light.
The light promotes self betterment.
Self betterment sanctifies the individual.
The sanctified individual converts the world to God.

Proceeding prudently through simple good will, the individual reaches the Divine Kingdom of the Light.

~ 67 ~

Ill Will

"Have nothing to do with the useless deeds of darkness" – Paul (Eph. 5:11)

Ill will leads to darkness.
Darkness fosters stagnancy.
Stagnancy preserves evil.
Evil enthrones idleness.
Idleness creates discord.
Discord awakens pride.
Pride awakens vanity.
Vanity stirs up base passions.
Base passions lead to a lack of discipline.
A lack of discipline keeps the heart hardened.
Hardness of heart imposes spiritual blindness.
Spiritual blindness leads to the abyss.

Surrendering to the unfruitful endeavors of incomprehension through simple ill will, human beings can roll indefinitely toward the abyss of darkness.

~ 68 ~

It Is Necessary to Wake Up

"Wake up, you who sleep; rise from the dead and Christ will shine on you." – Paul (Eph. 5:14)

A large number of both old followers and newcomers to Christian circles claim to have a very hard time understanding and applying the teachings of Jesus. Some find the texts to be obscure, while others persist in literary squabbles. They get upset; they protest and reject the divine bread, which is needed by the human envelope in order to remain on the earth.

Nevertheless, these friends are not even aware that this is happening. They remain asleep, victims of the paralysis of their higher faculties.

Significant, sanctifying divine invitations usually pass them by without being noticed. These distracted disciples see them as sacred events worthy of praise, but they soon forget all about them. The mind does not accept these invitations; it remains in a numbing sleep, incapable of analyzing or understanding.

People need to ask themselves what they are doing, what they want, what matters they are attending to, and for what ends they are destined. It is imperative to examine oneself, to emerge from animality and to arise to master one's own path.

Large, supposedly religious masses go through the events of each day like ranks of unconscious sleepwalkers. They talk about God, faith and spirituality as if they were living in the strange atmosphere of a dark nightmare. Shaken by the incessant currents of the river of life, they spin around in the eddy of events, blind, asleep and half dead until they awaken and get up through their own effort so that Christ may shine on them.

~ 69 ~

Today

But encourage one another every day, as long as it is called Today, so that none of you may be hardened by the deceitfulness of sin. – Paul (Heb. 3:13)

The Apostle's recommendation on daily mutual encouragement requires a great deal of reflection in order to keep doubts at bay.

Let us emphasize that Paul places singular importance on the time called "Today," pointing out the need to take advantage of the resources in play for the possibilities presented to us during the day at hand.

Many believe that in order to give advice to their brothers and sisters they must talk all the time, making themselves non-stop arguers. It is important to realize, however, that guidance consisting solely of words invariably leaves a great emptiness after they have been uttered.

As occurs in the realm of physical organizations, no spiritual edifice can be built without a foundation.

The statement, "But encourage one another" represents a more important appeal than simply calling one another to verbal duels.

Invitations and advice become more effective when accompanied by example. All those who practice the noble principles to which they have devoted themselves, who eagerly fulfill their duties, and who sincerely exhibit the good are exhorting their brothers and sisters in humanity to take the pathway of spiritual growth. It is to this kind of daily testimony that the Convert of Damascus invites us. Only by means of this constant practice of self betterment will men and women free themselves from deadly deceit.

Do not become hardhearted on the path that the Lord has led you to tread for your redemption, evolution and sanctification. Remember the importance of the time that is called "Today."

~ 70 ~

Praise

But he replied, "Instead, blessed are they who hear the word of God and obey it." – Jesus (Lk. 11:28)

Jesus was addressing the multitude with the enormous power of his love, winning everyone's attention. He had barely finished his loving and wise remarks, when a woman stood up in the crowd. Magnetized by his expression of sublime spirituality, she spoke in a loud voice about the blessings that would fall on Mary for having contributed to the coming of the Savior to earth. However, understanding perfectly well the unhappy consequences that could result from this thoughtless remark, the Master promptly responded that before anything else, blessed are they who, upon hearing God's revelation, put his teachings into practice and observe his principles.

The passage is a vivid clarification for sincere disciples not to let their campaign against personal praise weaken because such praise poisons their saintliest deeds and suffocates their purposes and hopes.

If you admire certain people who in your eyes appears to be a faithful worker for the good, do not bother them with words that the world has so frequently abused, constructing superficial phrases in the perilous feast of flattery. Help them with goodwill and understanding in carrying out the ministry they have been given, and do not forget that above all blessings shine the divine gifts of those who hear the Word of the Lord and put it into practice.

~ 71 ~

Shake the Dust Off

> *"And if no one welcomes you or listens to your words, then upon leaving that home or town, shake the dust off your feet."* – Jesus (Mt. 10:14)

The disciples materialized the teaching of Jesus by shaking the dust off their sandals upon leaving this or that rebellious or impenitent place. However, if the symbol portrayed in the Master's lesson were meant as only a mechanical gesture, we would have nothing more than a string of empty words.

The teaching is more profound, however. It recommends the elimination of unhealthy resentment.

Shaking the dust off one's feet means not holding on to any bitterness or pollutants in our lives due to the ignorance and perversity that appear on the path of our daily experiences.

It is natural to want to convey to others the seeds of truth and righteousness. However, if we are received with hostility, it would not be reasonable to continue with long observations and remarks which, instead of being conducive to success, create darkness and difficulties around us.

If you are not welcomed and your good intentions are not perceived, why waste time on accusations? Such an attitude cannot resolve spiritual problems. Are you not aware of the fact that those who deny and those who are indifferent will also be summoned by the death of the body to our homeland of origin? Lovingly entrust them to Jesus and proceed straight ahead in search of your sacred objectives. There is much to be done in the spiritual edification of the world and in your own selves. Therefore, shake off bad experiences and proceed joyfully.

~ 72 ~

Look Farther Ahead

"For with the same measure with which you measure others, you yourself shall be measured." – Jesus (Lk. 6:38)

To Eskimos, the sky is a continent made of ice, supported by seals.

To primitive peoples in the forest, there is no paradise greater than abundant game.

To persons of sectarian religion, the glory beyond the grave belongs exclusively to them and those who are of the same mind.

To the erudite, this world and the heavenly spheres that surround it are but a small corner of the universe.

Transfer this observation to your own field of daily activities and do not forget that external situations will be registered in your inner realm according to the elements of reflection harbored in your conscience.

If you persevere in anger, all the energies around you will appear enraged.

If you prefer sadness, you will see discouragement on every step of the road.

If you doubt yourself, no one will have confidence in your efforts.

If you have become accustomed to trouble and disagreement, it will be next to impossible for you to live in peace with yourself.

You will live either tormented or peaceful within a lower or higher realm, where you choose to place your mind. And within the atmosphere that suits you, you will live with the spirits you call upon. If you dwell on idleness, you will experience idleness in all its tones and hues; and if you involve yourself in work, you will find a thousand different ways of being useful.

The scenery that surrounds your steps will always be what you deem it to be, for with the same measure that you apply to Nature, the living work of God, Nature will measure you.

~ 73 ~

Let Us Learn as Quickly as Possible

So then, just as you received the Lord Jesus Christ, continue to live in him. – Paul (Col. 2:6)

Among those who refer to Jesus Christ, we can identify two large, distinct groups: those who know him through information, and those who have received his benefits. The former have gotten their knowledge about the Master from books or the exhortations of others, although they are on their way to becoming like the latter, who have already received his blessings. It is especially to this latter group that one should speak of the Gospel.

How do we find the Lord on our journey through the world? Sometimes, his divine presence manifests itself in the solution of a difficult human problem, in the restoration of bodily health, in the return of a loved one, in the spontaneous renewal of a common path so that new light dawns on one's mind.

There are many people who are well-informed about Jesus, and many have received his saving assistance.

It is imperative, however, that the beneficiaries of Christ's blessings feel as much joy in this gift as they feel in the pleasure of service and witness to the faith.

It is not enough for us to be showered with blessings. We must do our part in serving the Gospel by heeding its sanctifying plan.

Many tedious repetitions and much useless activity might be peculiar to minds that are merely informed; however, we who have received the infinite Mercy of the Lord should learn, as soon as possible, to adapt ourselves to his sublime will.

~ 74 ~

Bad Conversations

Do not be misled. Bad conversation corrupts good character. – Paul (I Cor. 15:33)

Undignified conversation always leaves traces of its inferiority wherever it has occurred. An environment of distrust immediately replaces the climate of serenity. The poison of unwholesome queries spreads rapidly. After unedifying conversation, there is always less sincerity and fewer expressions of fraternal strength. In its ignominious cradle are born the ghosts of slander that slip and slide amongst well-intentioned persons, trying to destroy honest homes; inferior preoccupations arise that spy from afar, twisting respectable attitudes; criminal curiosity emerges, appearing where it has not been called and emitting uncouth opinions that induce listeners to lies and insanity.

Bad conversation corrupts the most dignified thoughts. Worthy conversations everywhere suffer its implacable persecution, and it becomes imperative for people to guard against its insistent and destructive siege.

When the heart is given over to Jesus, it is very easy to control discussion topics and to eliminate dishonorable words.

Always examine the verbal inferences that surround your daily path. Have you heard accusations, bad news, frivolities and malicious gossip regarding others? Notice how you react. On every such occasion, there is a way for you to rectify it in a loving manner in Jesus Christ.

~ 75 ~

Complaining

Do everything without complaining or arguing. – Paul (Phil. 2:14)

There has never been an argument that was not preceded by complaining. It is an ancient habit of thoughtlessness to seek ingratitude, moral misery, pride, vanity and all the other scourges that ruin souls in this world in order to organize conversations of darkness, where goodness, love and truth are the focus of malice.

When someone begins to find little reasons to complain a lot, they should perform a rigorous self-examination to see if they are not suffering from the terrible illness of complaining.

Of course, those who are carrying out their duties on the list of righteous activities will not have time to complain.

The disciple must be on guard against accumulators of destructive energies, because, generally speaking, their pernicious influence has invaded nearly every corner of struggle on the planet.

They are easy to identify. For them, everything is wrong, nothing works, and one should not expect anything better in anything. Their speech is constantly irritable, and their remarks are unjust and discouraging.

Let us strive with all our might against these humiliating mental attitudes. Trusting in God, let us expand our hopes, and be assured that, as the old Proverb says, an optimistic heart is the medical prescription for peace and joy.

~ 76 ~

Witnesses

Therefore, since we too are surrounded by such a great cloud of witnesses, let us leave behind everything that hinders. – Paul (Heb. 12:1)

This concept of Paul of Tarsus deserves special consideration by students of the Gospel.

Each human existence is always an invaluable day of struggle – a generous step toward infinite ascension – and whatever their situation may be, people will always be surrounded by an enormous legion of witnesses. We are not only referring to those who are part of our own family circle, but above all, the friends and benefactors of each individual, who watch over him or her in the different situations of life from the lofty realms of higher spirituality.

All over the world, disciples are surrounded by a large cloud of spirit witnesses, who follow their every step, taking note of their attitudes, for no one has come to the earthly experience by chance, without solid reasons based on love or justice.

Generous spirits endorsed the requests of the repentant soul prior to its reincarnation; judges took part in the processes related to it, and friends interceded in the service of assistance, contributing to organizing the particulars of the redemptive struggle… These friends and guides steadfastly watch over their ward throughout the new task and *speak to him or her without words* in the innermost reaches of the conscience. Parents and children, husbands and wives, siblings and blood relatives of the world are the protagonists of the evolutionary drama, whereas these watchful observers usually remain on the other side of life.

This very day, do as much good as possible for your partners in the struggle, and do not forget those who, full of concern and love, watch over you in spirit.

~ 77 ~

To Respond

Let your conversation always be gracious, seasoned with salt so that you may know how to answer everyone. – Paul (Col. 4:6)

The act of responding beneficially to heterogeneous minds requires superior qualities that the individual should make an effort to acquire.

Points of view cannot be directed indiscriminately at fellow humans as they struggle with one another in evolutionary and redemptive tasks. It is necessary to address each one judiciously. One should not respond to someone working in the countryside by mentioning circumstances in the city. One should not use highly scientific remarks with someone complaining about the harshness of his or her individual path.

First of all, one must not be disagreeable to the listener; one should moderate the verbal attitude with a true grasp of life's problems. It is our duty to make our contribution so that those who have strayed away from simplicity and usefulness may realign themselves.

Every response in an important matter is like medicine: one must apply the dose with its effects in mind. Each individual will tolerate and benefit from the proper dosage. Even the solutions of truth and love must not be administered without this criterion. Applied in inappropriate doses, even the truth could destroy, just as love can cause damage...

Even if questioned by the greatest evildoer in the world, you should maintain a pleasant and dignified manner to inform or to enlighten. Knowing how to respond is a virtue from the sphere of celestial wisdom. For your own sake, do not forget the best way of caring for each individual.

~ 78 ~

According to the Flesh

For if you live according to the flesh, you will die. – Paul (Rom. 8:13)

For those who live according to the flesh, that is, according to the lower impulses, the season of earthly struggle is no more than a series of empty events.

At every moment, limitation will be an incessant phantom.

A mind overwhelmed with negativity will encounter death at every step.

For the conscience that has had the misfortune of espousing such dark concepts, human existence will be no more than a sad comedy.

Suffering will be seen as a house fit only for despair.

The work intended for spiritual purification will be experienced in a climate of rebelliousness.

Such a conscience cannot rely on the blessing of love, because, from its point of view, the ties of affection are mere mechanical accidents of fortuitous desires.

Pain – that benefactor and conservator of the world – becomes intolerable; discipline is an anguished prison, and service to others is downright humiliation.

The flesh never forgives; it does not know how to be selfless; it is pained whenever it has to yield to anyone, and when it is helpful, it demands from the recipient the subservience of a slave.

Wretched are they who live, breathe and act according to the flesh! The conflicts of possession torment their heart all the time with the force of the untamed life.

Woe to them, for the hour of renewal will always ring! If they have fled the atmosphere of immortality; if they have suffocated the best aspirations of their soul; if they have avoided the healthy exercise of suffering; if they have insisted on increasing their appetites and pleasures by complete integration with the "inferior side of life," what can they hope for at the end of their physical body except the grave, darkness and hopelessness in the cruelty of the night?

~ 79 ~

The "But" and Disciples

I can do everything through him who strengthens me. – Paul (Phil. 4:13)

Dedicated disciples affirm:

"Of myself, I possess nothing that is good, but Jesus will provide resources according to my needs."

"I don't have perfect knowledge of the way, but Jesus will guide me."

Lazy disciples declare:

"I don't disbelieve in the goodness of Jesus, but I don't have the strength for Christian work either.

"I know that the way is through Jesus, but the world won't let me follow him."

The former climb the mountain of resolution. They know their personal weaknesses, but they trust in the Divine Friend and choose to live according to his lessons.

The latter enjoy rest in the deep valley of their former life. They recognize the blessings the Master has conferred upon them, but they prefer to avoid them.

The former have set their mind on the Divine Light and press onward. The latter have stopped their thoughts on their own limitations.

The "but" is the conjunction that in our speech usually defines our inner position before the Gospel. When placed in front of the Sacred Name, it expresses firmness and trust, faith and valor; however, when placed after it, it expresses indecision and idleness, impermeability and indifference.

Only three letters denote our course.

"My principles recommend this, *but* Jesus asks for something else."

"Jesus advises me to do this, *but* I cannot."

Through one simple and small word, we profess our faith or confess our ineffectiveness.

Let us recall that, in spite of being stoned and persecuted, Paul of Tarsus could still affirm victoriously to the Philippians:

"I can do everything through him who strengthens me."

~ 80 ~

The "No" and the Struggle

"But let your yes be yes, and your no, no." – Jesus (Mt. 5:37)

Love in keeping with the teachings of the Gospel, but do not allow your love to become a shackle that hinders your progress toward the Higher Life.

Help all those who need your cooperation, but do not allow your assistance to foster trouble and vice on another's path.

Joyfully answer those who request a favor of you, but do not yield to frivolousness or foolishness.

Open the doors of well being to those around you, but do not overlook instructing your fellow incarnates about true happiness.

Cultivate graciousness and cordiality, but be loyal and sincere in your attitudes.

Saying "yes" can be very agreeable in every situation; however, saying "no" in certain circumstances of the human struggle is more constructive.

Trying to satisfy every request along the way means wasting time, and sometimes, life itself.

Just as "yes" should be spoken without flattering adulation, "no" should be uttered without harshness.

Quite often, it is necessary to say "no" so that true assistance is not lost. It is important to realize, however, that a healthy "no" never upsets. What hurts is the blunt tone in which it is spoken.

For the most part, manners speak louder than words.

"Let your yes be yes, and your no, no," recommends the Gospel. In saying either "yes" or "no", however, one does not have to come across as honey or bile. It will suffice to remember that Jesus is Master and Lord not only by what he does, but also by what he does not do.

~ 81 ~

In Paradise

Jesus answered him: "I tell you the truth, today you shall be with me in paradise." – Jesus (Lk. 23:43)

At first glance, it appears that Jesus addressed the so-called "good thief" out of individual sympathy.

But that is not the case.

In this lesson from Calvary, the Master gave a new definition of paradise.

In another passage, he said that the Divine Kingdom does not arise with outward appearances; rather, it is begun, developed and consolidated in eternal radiance within the heart.

In that hour of ultimate sacrifice, the good thief surrendered to Jesus Christ unconditionally. Readers of the Gospel are not aware of the challenging work and the new responsibilities that would weigh on his shoulders in order to cement his union with the Savior. They believe wholeheartedly that, from that moment forth, the former wrongdoer would enter heaven.

The symbol is beautiful and profound, and provides an idea of the infinite extent of the Divine Mercy.

In facing the truth, we can present ourselves with a voluminous baggage of debts from a dark past; however, from the instant we yield to the Lord's will by sincerely accepting the obligation of our own regeneration, we are headed for a different spiritual realm, where the yoke is easy and the burden is light. Upon reaching this point, the indebted spirit will not dwell in a false beatific attitude but will realize that, more than anything else, with Jesus suffering is rectification and crosses are immortal light.

That is why the good thief in that moment entered the lofty heights of paradise.

~ 82 ~

In Spirit

...but if through the spirit you mortify the deeds of the body, you shall live. – Paul (Rom. 8:13)

Those who live according to the sublime laws of the spirit breathe in a sphere different from the physical field in which they continue to walk.

An advanced comprehension denotes their inner condition.

They take advantage of the day like dedicated students who see their stay on the earth as an invaluable time of learning that should not be wasted.

In work, they discover the blessed gift of spiritual growth and improvement.

In the ignorance of others, they discover a precious opportunity to be of service.

In the difficulties and afflictions on the path, they gather resources for their own illumination and elevation.

They watch obstacles pass by as if they were clouds.

They love responsibilities, but do not become attached to possessions.

They administer with devotion, but stay clear of being controlling.

They support without unhealthy tendencies.

They serve without becoming enslaved.

They remain attentive to the need to sow, but do not worry about the harvest, for they know that the soil and the plant, the sun and the rain, the water and the wind belong to the Eternal Giver.

Beneficiaries of the divine gifts wherever they may be, they carry their personal treasures with them in their conscience and heart.

Blessed are those who go forth in spirit! For them, the affliction of death will be no more than the dawn of a new day, a sublime transformation and a joyous awakening!

~ 83 ~

According to Love

But if your brother is offended on account of your food, you are no longer acting according to love. Because of your food do not destroy him for whom Christ died. – Paul (Rom. 14:15)

Dogmatic prejudices have made victims in all eras, and the heirs of Christianity have not missed out on this concert of incomprehension.

Even today sectarian procedures, although less strict in their manifestations, continue to cause heartache and to disregard sentiments.

In another age, the adherents of Judaism quarreled violently about traditions regarding unclean food. Nowadays, we no longer face the issue of meat sacrifices in the Temple; nevertheless, new religious formalities have replaced the old reasons for argument and discord.

There are clergy who only feel like missionaries while performing the services they are responsible for, and there are believers who do not understand meditation and spiritualizing service except on Sunday morning while praying in a particular posture.

Disciples who have already succeeded in overcoming such barriers should cooperate in silence to extend the benefits of their victory.

It would be absurd to overcome this obstacle, and then deliberately continue with purely conventional displays, but it would also show a lack of charity to insult brothers and sisters who still face anguishing, inner mental conflicts before the august idea of God.

When you observe someone who is still prisoner of these illusions, remember that the Master went to the cross for him or her too. Put kindness ahead of analysis and your remark will be constructive and sanctifying. As long as there is understanding in the depths of your soul, you will find infinite resources for assistance, love and service.

~ 84 ~

Lifting up Holy Hands

Therefore, I want men to pray everywhere, lifting up holy hands without anger or contention. – Paul (1 Tim. 2:8)

In this passage from Paul's first epistle to Timothy, we receive a precious recommendation for service.

Some disciples will see in the text only an exhortation to a posture of praise; however, the Damascus convert explains that we should lift up holy hands everywhere without anger or contention.

Paul is not referring to the act of folding hands in prayer, which some people prefer to do in certain religious circles, where, due to the respectful artificiality of the situation, visible irritability or arguments are uncalled for. Rather, the Apostle is referring both to the honest and uplifting actions of individuals who cooperate with Divine Providence and to the daily work in the obscurest regions of the world.

In reading Paul's advice, we must remember that people, in their individual efforts, invariably lift their hands in their daily work. If they administrate, they point out ways to do things; if they participate in intellectual work, they use a pen; if they work in the field, they steer the farm implement. Paul adds, however, that such hands ought to be holy, meaning that even though many people lift their arms in their earthly work, it is important to discern its purpose and content.

If you wish to apply this reasoning to yourself, determine first of all else if your action is proceeding free of destructive anger and needless demands.

~ 85 ~

What about the Adulterer?

And placing her in their midst, they said to him, "Master, this woman was caught in the very act of adultery." (Jn. 8:4)

The case of this sinner presented to Jesus by the crowd involves highly significant considerations regarding people's tendency to see evil in others without seeing it in themselves.

Among the reflections suggested by the story, we may identify the erroneous concept of one-sided adultery.

If the misfortunate woman had been actually caught in the act, then where was the other adulterer? Why was he not brought for judgment? Was she the only one responsible? If there was a blemish on the collective organism requiring intervention in order to be eradicated, where was the one who had contributed to it hiding out?

The Master's attitude at that moment was characterized by infinite wisdom and unsurpassable love. Jesus could not place the weight of the blame on the unfortunate woman, and to help everyone grasp their error, he asked which of those present was without sin.

The long, spontaneous silence that followed was a more eloquent answer than any spoken statement could have been.

Standing with the woman were men who were sinners too, and who retreated in shame.

Man and woman come into the world with specific duties, which are to become part of an essentially unified task within the universal evolutionary plan. During the time of the earthly experience, one cannot fall without the other, because both have been given the same opportunity for sanctification.

If the women who have deviated from their elevated mission continue to be such an unfortunate focal point on the societal path, it is because male adulterers continue to be absent at the time of judgment, just as they were at the time of Jesus' famous suggestion.

~ 86 ~

Intending and Acting

Make direct pathways for your feet so that the lame may not be completely disabled but healed instead. – Paul (Heb. 12:13)

The well-intentioned individual will always make an effort to find a better pathway by nurturing higher ideals and leaning toward goodness and justice.

We must agree, however, that good intentions will be of little use if they are not connected to the sphere of immediate realities by correct actions.

It is necessary to focus on the good, but it is crucial to practice it.

Divine Providence covers people's road with material for their ongoing spiritual growth, making it possible for them to construct the "direct pathways" referred to by Paul of Tarsus. It is imperative for disciples to do so because the "lame" follow them on these pathways. Prisoners of ignorance and dishonesty crawl along them as best as they can as they near service of a higher order; and every now and then they approach Christ's faithful servants to suggest measures and activities in accordance with their lower mentality. Only those who have made straight pathways can escape their subtle assaults and defend themselves while offering these prisoners a new foundation so that they do not stray completely from the Divine Will.

Always apply your good intentions to the circle of practical realities in order for your good deeds to be illuminated with love, and in order for your love not to become an orphan of good deeds. Do this for yourself because you need to grow spiritually, and also for the lame who seek you out.

~ 87 ~

Always Ponder

And whatever you have heard me say in front of many witnesses, entrust to faithful men, who will then be able to teach others. – Paul (2 Tim. 2:2)

In Christian Spiritism, disciples of the Gospel often display unrepressed enthusiasm in their eagerness to spread a renewed, contagious and ardent faith. Nevertheless, such mental activity requires great caution, not only because admiration and wonder do not necessarily mean inner spiritual growth, but because it is crucial to know the qualities of the spiritual terrain to which the power of the knowledge is to be transmitted.

Of course, we are not referring to the basic act of sowing the revelatory truth or to the manifestation of fraternal kindness, both of which represent our natural duties in the good. Instead, we are suggesting the need for each brother and sister to watch over the treasure of spiritual gifts received from the higher realms, so that their heavenly qualities are not relegated to the contempt of evil or ignorance.

Let us spread the light of love with our companions on the journey, but let us also defend our inner sanctuary against the onslaughts of the darkness.

Let us remember that the Master himself had different lessons for the popular masses than for his small group of disciples. He did not include all of his disciples in his transfiguration on Tabor, and at the Last Supper he waited for Judas to leave before commenting on the anguishes that were to follow.

We must pay attention to these attitudes of Christ and know that not everything is meant for everybody. The ennobled spirits that communicate with the physical realm always adopt a selective criterion as they look for capable and faithful individuals who are suited to teach others. If these spirits can use their illuminated sight to identify problems, and thus act wisely regarding them, how much more careful should disciples who only see with their physical eyes be? Let us work on behalf of all by holding out fraternal hands to them, but let us also understand that each person stands on his or her own rung on the infinite ladder of life.

~ 88 ~

Discipline

If you are enduring discipline, God is treating you as his children; for what child is not disciplined by his father? – Paul (Heb. 12:7)

Blessed is the spirit who understands the Lord's discipline and accepts it without resistance.

However, few individuals manage to understand and bear discipline.

At times, a generous reprimand from the Most High – the symbol of unbridled love – reaches the human arena as a sacred and silent warning. Nevertheless, on most occasions, the incarnate mind deflects the salvific prod, immerses itself in the night of rebelliousness, disregards valuable possibilities, and labels as an unbearable misfortune the renewing influence meant to brighten the sad, dark road.

When confronted with this regenerative phenomenon, many people opt for a spectacular escape from the difficult situation and defenselessly give in to a slow suicide, abandoning themselves to complete indifference toward their destiny.

Those who proceed in such a way cannot be treated as children, since they have isolated themselves and have turned away from Divine Providence by erecting dense walls of darkness between their own heart and the Father's blessings.

Those who understand the discipline of the All Merciful readjust themselves in a new and promising circle of life.

Once the inner storm is overcome, they re-evaluate opportunities for learning, serving and constructing, and based on the bitter experiences of yesterday, they apply the benefits of the Higher Life with an eye on tomorrow.

Do not forget that evil cannot correct anyone. When the Lord's discipline reaches you on your path, accept it humbly and know that it is a true message from heaven.

~ 89 ~

The Beatitudes

"Blessed are you when men hate you, when they exclude you, harm you and reject your name as evil on account of the Son of Man." – Jesus (Lk. 6:22)

The problem of the beatitudes requires serious thought before it can be seen as a resolved issue in the area of understanding.

Jesus confers the credential of blessedness on followers who share in his afflictions and service; nevertheless, we must point out that the Master regards sacrifice and suffering as instructive and redemptive blessings.

Thus, it is crucial to be able to accept them.

This or that person will be blessed for having brought goodness into the midst of material poverty, for finding happiness in simplicity and peace, and for knowing how to maintain a durable and divine hope in his or her heart.

But… what does sincere adherence to the sacred obligations of such a designation entail?

In the guidance that characterizes his teachings, the Master is referring to the eternal beatitudes; however, there are few who approach them with the full understanding of someone who is approaching an immense treasure. If visited by pain, most of the less-favored on the earthly plane would rather complain and despair; if invited to demonstrate self-denial, they make improper demands, and instead of working peacefully, they lose themselves in the unworthy enterprises of unbridled ambition.

Jesus offers many beatitudes. Only a rare few, however, really want them. That is why there are many poor and afflicted people who are in dire need in the world, but who are not yet blessed in heaven.

~ 90 ~

The Divine Worker

"His winnowing fork is in his hand; he will clear his threshing floor and will gather the wheat into his barn, but he will burn up the chaff with unquenchable fire." – John the Baptist (Lk. 3:17)

Ever since the earliest organizations of the gospel movement, apostles and followers of Christ have referred to him by many names.

Jesus has been called Master, Shepherd, Messiah, Savior and Prince of Peace. All these titles are just and venerable; however, we must not forget that alongside these sublime invocations lies the Baptist's unexpected description. The Precursor calls Jesus an industrious worker whose winnowing fork is in his hand, and who will clear the hard and rough floor, gather the wheat at the proper time, and purify the chaff with the unquenchable flame of justice and love.

It is interesting to note that John does not introduce the Lord as someone who is holding parchments, filled with laws and regulations in his hands, nor does he refer to him according to the old Judaic traditions that expected the Divine Messenger to arrive in a chariot of magnificent glory. Instead, he refers to an optimistic, self-sacrificing worker. A rustic winnowing fork is not at his side but is ready in his hands, and in his spirit reigns the hope of cleansing the earth that has been entrusted to his saving directives.

All of you, who are pursuing earthly endeavors to make things better, keep your devotion to the cause of the Christ's Gospel lit in your souls. Let us not be waylaid by difficulties or ingratitude. Let us carry out our activities with the precious stimulus of faith, because ahead of us, blessing our humble cooperation, is that Divine Worker who will clear the threshing floor of the world.

~ 91 ~

That's Your Problem

And he [Judas] said, "I have sinned by betraying innocent blood." But they responded, "What is that to us? That's your problem." (Mt. 27:4)

The word of human evil is always cruel to those who listen to its criminal insinuations.

The case of Judas demonstrates the irresponsibility and wickedness of all those who perpetrate grave wrongs.

If the incautious spirit listens to evil suggestions, it will soon become aware of the loneliness that surrounds it in the sphere of unfortunate consequences.

Those who act uprightly will discover that the happy results of their initiative yields a flood of friends who want to share in their victories; on the other hand, they will rarely find anyone who wants to share in their afflictions on days of temporary defeat.

Such a reality should lead one to be more cautious.

Most people repeat Judas' bitter experience every day, although in a different manner.

There are those who listen to the offensive insinuations of malice or disobedience regarding their inner tranquility, family matters and daily work. Sometimes, people live peacefully as they carry out their duties; however, envious or despairing suggestions reach them and they get confused by erroneous perspectives and inadvertently enter mazes of darkness and ingratitude. When they realize the error of their heart or mind, they anxiously return to their counselors of the day before; however, reiterating Judas' remark, they mockingly ask, "What is that to us? That's your problem."

92

God Does Not Forsake

I have given her time to repent of her prostitution, but she has not. (Rev. 2:21)

Even though the Book of Revelation is replete with profound symbolism, that should not keep us from examining its content and extracting lessons amenable to increasing our spiritual progress.

This verse from Revelation provides us with an idea of the generosity of the Most High regarding the wrongs and defections of his transgressing children.

Many people insist that the divine determinations are unbending and irrevocable; however, we must recognize that hearts inclined to such a point of view are not yet aware of the sublime essence of the love that erases dark debts and causes a new day to dawn on the horizons of the soul.

If earthly judges are capable of fraternal dispositions such as granting probation, how could the heavenly court consist of harsher and more inflexible minds?

The Father's House is much more generous than any image of magnanimity presented thus far by religious thought. In its abundant granaries there are loans and moratoriums, concessions of time and resources that the liveliest human imagination could hardly conceive.

The Almighty supplies gifts to all, and nowadays people should ponder the resources granted to them by heaven for repentance and seek to renew themselves on the path of the good.

The prisoners of the idea that God's justice is implacable ignore the Almighty's powerful aid, manifested in a thousand different ways; however, those who seek their personal illumination through universal love know that God always provides and that it is necessary to learn how to receive.

~ 93 ~

The Gospel and Woman

Likewise, husbands should love their wives as their own bodies. He who loves his wife loves himself. – Paul (Eph. 5:28)

Many times, the Apostle to the Gentiles has been accused of being overly severe toward woman. In certain passages of his letters to the early churches, Paul sets forth austere measures which, to some extent, have been shocking to many disciples. However, few have been able to glean the use of Christ's resources from his forceful words in order to strengthen the protection of woman as well as her opportunities for spiritual growth.

True feminism actually started with Jesus; not the kind that puts colored banners of the world's political ideologies in the hands of its advocates, but the kind that instills lofty and holy directives in their hearts.

In the stricter circles of religious faith such as in Judaism before the Master arrived, woman was little more than enslaved property. Even prominent figures such as David and Solomon were not exempt from the abuses of their time in this respect.

The Gospel, however, begins a new era for women's hopes. In it we see the consecration of the Most-Holy Mother, the sublime conversion of Mary Magdalene, the dedication of Lazarus's sisters and the selfless spirit of the women of Jerusalem who followed the Lord up to the last moment. Ever since Jesus, we have seen an increasing respect for woman's mission. Paul of Tarsus was the consolidator of this regenerative movement. Despite his stern words, he sought to lift woman up from her abased condition, entrusting her to man as a mother, sister, wife or daughter, with a common destiny and as a child of God, like himself.

~ 94 ~

Sex

I know and am certain in the Lord Jesus that nothing is unclean in itself except to the one who regards it as such. – Paul (Rom. 14:14)

When Paul of Tarsus wrote this remark to the Romans, he was referring to the food that at that time represented an object of bitter dispute between Gentiles and Jews.

Nowadays, the act of eating does not incite perilous arguments, but we can take this verse and project it onto other areas of erroneous opinions.

Let us take sex, for instance. No other area of earthly activity has suffered greater defamation. Fundamentally blind of spirit, humans in general have not yet managed to discover in sex one of the most sublime reasons for their existence. The most exquisite achievements in the planetary realm, such as the uniting of souls for motherhood and fatherhood, the creation and the reproduction of bodies, the extension of life and the precious stimuli for work and regeneration, have been provided by the Lord to his creatures by means of sexual emotions; however, humans have desecrated this "holy place," populating its altars with the ghosts of licentiousness.

Sex established the home and created the name "mother," but humans in their selfishness exchanged it for absurd animalistic experiences, thereby generating cruel trials for themselves.

The Father offered this sanctuary to his children, but a lack of understanding is what they have offered in return. That is why painful and distressing dramas are being played out on every continent on earth.

Even so, immersed in deplorable distortions, people demand sexually instructive programs. Yes, such programs might be useful, but only when the holy notion of the divinity of this creative power is more widespread, for as long as uncleanliness remains in the heart of those who analyze or teach, such methods will be nothing more than uncleanliness as well.

~ 95 ~

This Is the Message

For this is the message you have heard from the beginning: Let us love one another. (1 Jn. 3:11)

All over the world we feel a tremendous longing for new messages from heaven. The dynamic forces of thought insist on receiving modern expressions of old truths, and this provides opportunities for different mental creations. We can see, however, that art, in seeking new expressions, is populated with negative images; that politics, in creating ideologies and new processes for governing, expands the course of destructive war; and that science, in seeking to soar ever higher, invents theories that impinge on harmony and well-being.

The great branches of religion are making a gallant effort to demonstrate the eternality of life by beseeching spectacular signs from the invisible realm for ordinary people.

We must agree that the lofty aspirations of the human spirit are always useful when it truly seeks expressions of a divine nature. However, we must also agree that even though there are countless substantial, spiritually constructive and illuminating messages on earth, the greatest and most invaluable of all ever since the beginning of the planet's organization has been that of fraternal solidarity in "Let us love one another."

This is a fundamental recommendation. By understanding its meaning, each disciple can examine, in life's daily circle of struggle, the level of understanding that he or she already possesses regarding the Divine Plan.

Even if this or that brother or sister has not yet grasped its meaning, begin exercising this fatherly recommendation yourself.

Love always. Do all the good you can. Start by appreciating those who do not understand you, knowing that they will make you a better person more quickly.

~ 96 ~

Precisely because of This

I have not written to you because you do not know the truth, but because you do know it. (1 Jn. 2:21)

The increasingly intense interchange between "the living" and "the dead" comprises a great event for evangelical organizations in general.

It is not solely an accomplishment for the Spiritist school; it belongs to the entire Christian community.

We continue to see protests by organized dogmatism, but the revivification of the truth requires such to be the case.

Every acquisition has a price and every renewal will meet immediate opposition.

The day will come when the many subdivisions of evangelicalism will grasp the divine purpose of this new order of things.

The movement of spirit-related exchange between the two spheres is growing wider each day. The devotion of discarnates is drawing the attention of incarnates.

The Lord has permitted a worldwide Pentecost for readjustment to the eternal reality.

It is noteworthy, however, that the touching and reinvigorating voices from the Other Side usually repeat age-old formulas of the Revelation, and they recall the past of earthly wisdom in order to extract more respectable concepts about life.

It is at this point that we remember John's words and ask sincerely: Do the "dead" really communicate with the "living"? If so, why are people unaware of this truth?

They are not.

If the departed once again speak to those who remain behind, it is because the latter do, in fact, know the way of redemption through Jesus, but they are neither motivated nor determined to follow it.

~ 97 ~

Keep the Model

Hold to the standard of sound teaching. –
Paul (2 Tim. 1:13)

Spread the resources that Providence has entrusted into your industrious hands, but do not forget that a comforting word to the afflicted represents an effort straight from your heart in the sowing of the good.

Bread for the body is an act of charity for which you will be rightly compensated, but a friendly smile is a blessing that will last forever.

Send messengers to offer fraternal assistance, but do not overlook visiting ailing brothers and sisters now and then to listen to them in person.

A group effort to provide assistance is a gesture that will win appreciation for you, but your direct assistance in helping the needy will prepare you spiritually to face your own battles.

Mount the dais and teach the path of redemption to all, but take a break from your lecturing every now and then in order to listen to the sorrows of a fellow companion in the human experience, even if they are the offspring of despair or ignorance, so that you do not lose your sense of proportion as you progress.

Cultivate the flowers in the private garden of your dearest relationships, because apart from the flowerbed of experience, it is very difficult to attend to the noble and intensive tilling of the soil. However, do not regularly flee the human forest, afraid of the vermin and monsters that live in it, for it is crucial that you prepare yourself to advance later on in its midst.

In the circles of life, do not forget the need for the teaching to be engraved within you.

Just as you cannot get your individual nourishment through someone else or learn a lesson by storing it in someone else's memory, you will not be able to present yourself to the Supreme Powers of Wisdom and Love by way of accomplishments and victories that you have not lived or achieved yourself.

Thus, "Hold to the standard of sound teaching."

~ 98 ~

Avoid Quarrels

And the Lord's servant must not quarrel. –
Paul (2 Tim. 2:24)

Avoid those who look for quarrels as they serve the Lord.

They are not in search of divine clarity for the heart. They simply argue over praise and prominence in the arena of fleeting circumstances. As they study the sacred scriptures, they do not draw from them the resources they need for personal illumination but rather the means they need for personal recognition. They oppose those who do not adopt their personal ideas; they are against endeavors that do not allow them direct control; they do not cooperate except from the top down; nor do they see usefulness in any tasks that they themselves are not in charge of. They love long arguments over where to put a comma, and they waste countless days finding the apparent contradictions among writers dedicated to the ideals of Jesus. They never find time for work that entails Christian humility, because they are only interested in their own personal recognition. They regard the conjugation of the verbs to help, to forgive and to serve as odd. They invariably fixate on humankind's imperfections and they criticize simply out of the bad habit of finding fault. They quarrel over all the particulars of evangelical edification, and when the possibility for constructive agreement appears, they come up with new ways to cause trouble.

Those who adhere to the Redeeming Gospel out of a spirit of contention are the greatest and subtlest adversaries of the Kingdom of God.

It is crucial for disciples to be on the lookout so that they do not lose themselves in the folly of acerbic and useless words.

We were not called upon to quarrel but to serve and to learn with the Master; nor were we called upon to enthrone the "self" but to fulfill the supreme designs of building the Divine Kingdom within us.

~ 99 ~

With Ardent Love

But above all, show ardent charity toward one another. – (1 Pet. 4:8)

It is not enough to proclaim virtue on behalf of establishing the Divine Kingdom among humankind.

Problem excessively debated – solution more delayed…

Let each one of us personally listen to the apostolic warning and be filled with ardent charity for one another.

To speak well, to teach accurately and to believe sincerely are the first steps of service. It is crucial to work, act and feel with Christ.

Fraternity that is simply suggested to others merely builds a fine facade that experience can burn down in one minute.

It is urgent for us to get at the substance, the essence...

Let us be understanding towards the ignorant, watchful towards those who have gone astray in evil and darkness, patient towards those who are ill, serene towards the irritable, and above all, let us display kindness towards all those whom the Master has entrusted to us for the lessons of each day.

The ability to think quickly and act daringly may be a valuable asset, but if it lacks the heart to sense problems, to deal with them and to resolve them for the common good, it is easily susceptible to becoming a calculator.

Let us not hold ourselves back with compassion that is merely theoretical.

Let us seek fraternal, spontaneous, ardent and pure love.

Heavenly charity not only spreads benefits. It also radiates the Divine Light.

~ 100 ~

Let Us Give Thanks

In everything give thanks, for this is God's will for you in Christ Jesus. – Paul (1 Thes. 5:18)

The stone secures.
The thorn forewarns.
Bile heals.
Fire recasts.
Refuse fertilizes.
The storm purifies the atmosphere.
Suffering redeems.
Illness warns.
Sacrifice enriches life.
Death always renews.

Let us learn, therefore, to praise the Lord for the blessings he bestows on us.

Good is the heat that modifies; good is the cold that preserves.

The joy that stimulates is the sister of the pain that perfects.

Let us pray to Heavenly Providence for enough light for our eyes to identify the granary of grace in which we find ourselves.

It is our inner blindness that causes us to trip over obstacles, wherein only divine favor dwells.

And especially, when we enunciate a worthy desire, let us prepare to welcome the lessons that will help us accomplish it according to the superior purposes that govern our destiny.

Let us not be frightened by unforeseen difficulties or dolorous circumstances.

Help from Above does not always appear in the form of heavenly delight.

It usually appears in the form of a less desirable resource. Let us remember, however, that someone in danger of drowning in the deep waters that cover the abyss can be saved only at the price of extreme measures.

So, let us give thanks for all the experiences along our evolutionary pathway, on our sanctifying search for the Divine Will in Jesus Christ, our Lord.

~ 101 ~

Resist Temptation

Blessed is the man who endures temptation. (Js. 1:12)

As our spiritual ship sails through the waters of inferiority, we are not immune to severe inner conflicts. Especially in the physical realm, whenever we undertake the improvement of our soul by making use of the work and obstacles presented by the world, we can expect an increase in the difficulties that confront us on the path of illuminated knowledge.

Against our yearning for enlightenment, we are faced with past millennia of darkness. Opposing our most humble aspirations to grow in the good, there are centuries in which we took pleasure in evil.

Hence, amongst the blessings from On High, temptations of all sorts abound on the disciple's path.

At times, disciples believe they are well-prepared to slay the dragons of animality that prowl about their doors; however, when they least expect it, degrading suggestions pounce on them again and drive them into the challenging battle.

Therefore, it is obvious that not even the grave can exonerate us from our duels with the darkness because its roots extend into the very organization of our spirit. Only the death of our inner imperfection can free us from them.

So, constructive tolerance should envelop the human pathway because evil insinuations are going to encircle us roundabout as long as we linger in our partial accomplishment of the good.

We will achieve freedom only when we attain full enlightenment.

Understanding the transcendent importance of this fact, the Apostle states, "Blessed is the man who endures temptation." At the present time, any reference to complete triumph is impossible because we are still so very far from the angelic state. However, we will be blessed if we endure well these types of struggles and control the impulses of undeveloped sentiments, perfecting them little by little at the cost of our personal effort so that we may not give in defenselessly to the inferior suggestions that seek to turn us into living instruments of evil.

~ 102 ~

Caesar and Us

And Jesus answered them saying, "Then give to Caesar what is Caesar's and to God what is God's." (Mk. 12:17)

All over the world, according to their own merits, people will always encounter the figure of Caesar symbolized by the secular government.

Evil individuals will obviously produce evil politicians.

Idle and indifferent collectivities will face disorganized administrations.

In any case, Caesar's influence will surround the individual and demand the fulfillment of material obligations.

It is imperative to give him what is his.

The student of the Gospel should not invoke religious principles or individual idealism to shun these obligations.

If there are errors in the laws, let us remember the extent of our individual debts to Divine Providence, and let us cooperate with the human governing body by offering our good will and our participation in its duties, aware that our disinterest or rebelliousness will not resolve its problems.

It is preferable for disciples to sacrifice themselves and suffer rather than lag behind regarding the respectable laws that temporarily govern them on the physical plane, whether through disobedience towards the established principles or through excessive enthusiasm that tempts them to advance too rapidly for their time.

Are there iniquitous decrees?

Try to remember if you have been cooperating with those who govern your material landscape.

Live in harmony with your superiors and do not forget that the best position is that of balance.

If you intend to live correctly, do not give Caesar the vinegar of your sour criticism. Assist him with your efficient work in the healthy desire to do right, convinced that he and we are children of the same God.

~ 103 ~

The Cross and Discipline

And they compelled a certain Simon of Cyrene, the father of Alexander and Rufus, who was passing by, to carry the cross. (Mk. 15:21)

Many students of Christianity resist thinking about the cross, alleging that reminders of Calvary are an undue worship of suffering.

They assert that the memory of the Master between common thieves at the time of the crucifixion is negative.

However, we belong to those who prefer to look at all of Christ's days as glorious journeys and all of his minutes as divine fractions of his sacred ministry in light of the needs of the human soul.

Every hour of his presence amongst his creatures is clothed in striking beauty, and the instant of the shameful cross is replete with symbolic majesty.

Many disciples have a lot to say about the cross of the Lord, and they tend to examine with theoretical particulars the imaginary crosses they bear.

However, only those who have gained the strength to deny themselves so as to follow in the footsteps of the Divine Master have really shouldered the redemptive cross that is their responsibility to bear.

Many people confuse discipline with spiritual illumination. Only after accepting the gentle yoke of Jesus Christ can we raise to our shoulders the cross that will grant us spiritual wings for the life eternal.

Against the nearly-always idle arguments of those who have not yet truly understood the sublimity of the cross, let us observe the example of the man from Cyrene during the Savior's culminating moments. Christ's cross was the most beautiful cross in the world; nonetheless, the man who assisted him did not do so of his own volition, but instead obeyed an indeclinable order. Even today, most men and women accept the obligations inherent to their own duties because they are forced to.

~ 104 ~

A Sacred Right

For regarding Christ, it has been granted to you not only to believe in him but also to suffer for him. – Paul (Phil. 1:29)

To collaborate personally and directly with human administrators has always been the ambition of workers of this or that earthly organization.

The sharing of responsibilities between the superior who knows how to decide and do what is right and the subordinate who knows how to serve is an act of invariable trust that establishes the basis for harmony in daily activities and is an accomplishment that all institutions seek to attain.

Many disciples of Christianity seem to be unaware of the fact that, in relation to Jesus, this reciprocity is the same but raised to the highest degree through faithfulness and understanding.

A greater understanding of the divine plan means a greater expression of individual witness in the Master's service.

Expanded competence – increased duties.

More light – more sight.

Many individuals have naturally gained certain intellectual qualities but they are still mentally infirm. They would like to accept the Savior and believe in him, but they cannot attain such inner spiritual growth right away. Because of the ignorance that they have not yet eradicated and the capriciousness that they still cherish, they cannot yet distinguish the truths of Jesus. They must readjust themselves in order for this to happen.

However, disciples who have accepted the benefits of faith are considered worthy of living spiritually with the Master. Between the Lord and them there is already a sharing of trust and responsibility. As long as the joys of Bethlehem and the glories of Capernaum abound, the labor of faith unfolds marvelously; however, once the anguish of the cross appears, many disciples flee in fear of suffering, revealing themselves unworthy of their choice. Those who behave like this may be regarded as mad because to withdraw from cooperating with Christ is to scorn a sacred right.

~ 105 ~

The Primordial Remark

Jesus answered him, "The first of all the commandments is: Hear, O Israel; the Lord is our God; the Lord is one. (Mk. 12:29)

On replying to the scribe that had questioned him concerning the first of all the commandments, Jesus precedes the initial article of the Decalogue with an original remark that merits a closer look.

Before all of the laws of Moses, the revelations of the Prophets and his own redeeming blessings in the Gospel, the Master sets a forceful declaration of principles that beckons all minds to the plane of substantial unity. Consolidating the saving work that he himself brought from the highest realms, Christ proclaims to humankind that there is only one Almighty Lord: the Father of Infinite Mercy.

He knew beforehand that many would not accept the truth; that many would try to escape their just obligations; that there would be delays, ill will, indifference and laziness regarding the Good Tidings. Nonetheless, he upheld the divine unity so that all disciples would realize that they could poison their own freedom, create fictitious gods, raise discord, temporarily betray the Law, stand still on their path, and carry out war and destruction, but they would never be able to deceive the eternal truths, to which all will adjust themselves one day in the perfect understanding that "The Lord is our God; the Lord is one."

~ 106 ~

There Is a Big Difference

Then Peter said, "I have neither silver nor gold, but what I do have I give to you." (Acts 3:6)

It is right to recommend much caution to those who are interested in the advantages of human politics, and who use references to Jesus and the Gospel to explain certain absurdities in matters of social theory.

Nearly always, human law addresses the governed by using this formula: "Whatever you have belongs to me."

Christianity, however, through Peter's inspired lips, proclaims to all: "Whatever I have, I have given to you."

Have you ever thought about how great the world will be when men and women decide to give what they possess for the construction of universal evolution?

In ordinary charity work at public charitable institutions, individuals rarely offer to their neighbor what may be regarded as their own intrinsic qualities.

Could anyone base genuine service to the eternal good entirely on the perishable possessions of earth?

Generous individuals may distribute money and useful things to the needy on their path, but they will not kindle within themselves the light and joy that are born from these gifts if they do not give them with a sentiment of love, which, in essence, is their imperishable and true wealth.

Everyone brings with them the worthy qualities that they have already attained, and which enable them to continue to advance in the realm of spiritual acquisitions of a higher order.

Do not forget the loving words of Peter; give of yourself in your endeavor of salvation, for those who are waiting for gold or silver in order to perform good deeds are truly still very far from the ability to help themselves.

~ 107 ~

Compassion

But compassion with contentment is a great gain. – Paul (1 Tim. 6:6)

Much is said about compassion, but when we make references to this virtue, it is hard to distinguish between compassion and lowering oneself.

"I'll help this man but he's an addict."

"I'll help this woman but she's ignorant and bad."

"I'll take pity on this brother but he's cruel and ungrateful."

"I feel for this person but he's no good."

Such statements are repeated all the time by lips that claim to be Christian.

In fact, on earth we normally encounter only the compassion that is comprised of a soft voice and thorny hands.

It dispenses honey and poison.

It puts balm on wounds and then tears them open.

It extends open arms and charges payment for recognition.

It rescues and then pummels.

It supports and then discourages.

It offers kind words and then hurls hostile retorts.

It appeases the hunger of life's travelers with loaves full of bile.

True compassion, however, is the daughter of love.

It wastes no time pointing out evil.

It is concerned too much with the good to trade it for trifles and it knows that each minute in the economy of life is precious.

The Gospel does not refer to the false compassion that is full of illusions and demands. Those who display enough strength to embrace the Christian life find the resources to assist joyfully. They do not get caught in the web of destructive criticism, and they know how to sow the good, water its seeds, tend to its shoots and await its fruitage.

Paul tells us that "compassion with contentment" is a "great gain" for the soul, and honestly, we know of no other that can bring more prosperity to the heart.

~ 108 ~

Prayer

Persevere in prayer, being watchful in it with thanksgiving. – Paul (Col. 4:2)

Many believers would like to use prayer as if it were a broom or a hammer.

They expect immediate results, unaware of any preparatory effort. Others persevere in prayer, but remain frightened and anxious. They wear themselves out and consume valuable energy on unjustifiable afflictions. They see only evil and darkness, and they never take time to examine the tender young sprout of the Divine Seed or the close or remote potential for the good. They imprison themselves on the "evil side," and sometimes waste an entire lifetime without any intention of going over to the "good side."

What probability of success could possibly be in store for the needy who cry out their appeals with obvious symptoms of imbalance? From the very start, a sensible grantor will hold off on an answer, prudently waiting for the potential grantee to regain his or her composure.

In this sense, Paul's words are clear.

It is imperative to persist in prayer, to be watchful in it with thanksgiving. It is crucial to realize that praise does not only entail uttering beautiful words. It also means being happy while in full combat for the victory of the good, expressing gratitude to the Lord for the reasons for suffering and sacrifice, and seeking the advantages that adversity and effort have brought to the spirit.

Let us ask Jesus for the gift of peace and happiness, but let us not forget to glorify his sublime designs each time his merciful and just will clashes with our inferior objectives. Let us be convinced that ill-timed prayer, comprised of desperate thoughts and improper demands, is destined for the soil of renewal, as happens to an unproductive flower blown away by the wind.

~ 109 ~

Three Musts

> *"Thus I say to you: ask and it shall be given to you; seek and you shall find; knock and the door shall be opened to you."* – Jesus (Lk. 11:9)

Ask, seek, knock…

These three musts recommended by Jesus were not spoken without special meaning.

In the tangle of the struggles and debts of the earthly experience, it is crucial for people to learn to ask for a pathway to freedom from the old chains of suffocating conventions, sterile prejudices, empty devotions and unbreakable habits. It is necessary to vehemently and decisively desire to get out of the dark thicket in which most individuals have lost sight of the eternal interests.

Immediately thereafter, it is imperative to seek.

Seeking consists of selective effort. The field is loaded with inferior attractions, some of which are adorned with luring appeal. It is crucial to find the worthy and sanctifying way to act. Many run after dangerous mirages, like moths fascinated with the light of the fire. They come from far away, get too close to the flame and consume the blessing of their body.

It is imperative to learn to seek what is truly good.

Once the spiritually constructive path is established, the time comes to knock on the door of spiritual growth. Without the mallet of methodical effort and without the chisel of goodwill, it is extremely difficult to sculpt the resources of the corporeal life into luminous works of divine art meant for spiritual happiness and eternal love.

It is not enough, therefore, to pray without direction, to seek without examination, and to act without a lofty objective.

Let us ask the Lord to free us from primitive animality. Let us seek the realm of sublime spirituality and work for our place within it in order to make ourselves faithful instruments of the Divine Will.

Ask, seek, knock!... This trilogy of Jesus holds a special meaning for students of the Gospel in every era.

~ 110 ~

Personal Magnetism

And the entire crowd tried to touch him because from him came a power that healed everybody (Lk. 6:19)

Nowadays, we are quite astonished to see a group of eminent spiritualists spreading concepts related to personal magnetism as if we were witnessing a novelty from the 19th century.

This work of investigating and disseminating secret human powers comprises an invaluable aid in both present and future educational endeavors; however, it is important to remember that this spiritual endeavor is nothing new.

During his passage on this planet, Jesus was the individualized sublimation of personal magnetism in its substantially divine expression. People competed for his enchanting presence and the crowds followed him, touched with singular admiration. Nearly everybody sought to touch his clothing. Radiations of love emanated from him, neutralizing recalcitrant illnesses. The Master spontaneously produced a climate of peace that reached anyone who enjoyed his presence.

Thus, if you seek an easier way for the full blossoming of your psychic potential, it is reasonable to take advantage of the experiences that earthly guides offer you, but do not forget the examples and living demonstrations of Jesus.

If you intend to attract, it is imperative to know how to love. If you desire true influence on earth, sanctify yourself through the influence of heaven.

~ 111 ~

Win Friends

"Moreover, I tell you: use unjust wealth to win friends...." – Jesus (Lk. 16:9)

If people could study the remotest past of their human experience, they would quickly realize that all the knowledge- and health-related opportunities that make them happy come from the Divine Goodness, and that most of the material resources at the mercy of their whims proceed from injustice.

It is not up to us to particularize, but to realize that concepts regarding human rights are the result of divine influence; however, we are also compelled to realize how slow our personal evolution from downright selfishness to universal love, from iniquity to true justice has been.

In this regard, we must remember that nearly all the countries on earth arose centuries ago as the result of cruel conquests. With a few exceptions, humans have proved to be wasteful servants, who, at the time of accountability, cannot show that they have been worthy of stewardship.

That is why Jesus bequeathed the parable of the unfaithful servant to us, inviting us to true fraternity so that through it we may find the road to rehabilitation.

The Master told us to win friends, that is, to expand the circle of affections in which we feel more and more intensively aided by the spirit of cooperation and intercessory resources.

If our spiritual life has been somber and painful, let us seek to simplify it by acquiring true friendships, which will assist us on the difficult ascent to redemption. Even if today we do not have strong connections with the riches of injustice, we did yesterday, and it is crucial that we take advantage of this time for our own individual readjustment before Divine Justice.

~ 112 ~

Eternal Tabernacles

> *"Moreover, I tell you: use unjust wealth to win friends, so that when it is gone, they may welcome you into eternal tabernacles."* – Jesus (Lk. 16:9)

Those who are unaware of their spiritual obligations will think that this verse refers to a smart crook who buys the favors of corrupt officials in order to win honorable titles of human convention. However, when Jesus speaks of friends, he is referring to sincere and devoted brothers and sisters. When he mentions unjust wealth, he is including the individual's entire past, with all of its pain-filled lessons. Likewise, when he refers to eternal tabernacles, he is not locating them in the heavenly courts.

The Master located the sacred tabernacle in the human heart.

More than anyone else, the Savior was familiar with our imperfections; and displaying immense compassion toward the deficiencies that mark our spirits, he uttered these divine words for us to examine.

Cognizant of our errors, he is essentially saying that we should use our temporary wealth for true fraternity so that by forgetting our past crimes and hatreds, we may become one another's selfless brothers and sisters.

Therefore, incarnate or discarnate, let us value our work while on earth by using all the resources available for our own improvement and the edification of our neighbor, acting in accordance with the light and loving at all times. By living according to such norms of sublime solidarity, we can always count on the dedication of faithful friends, who, being more dedicated and ennobled disciples than we are, will be able to assist us effectively by welcoming us into their hearts, the tabernacles of the Lord. They will not only help us obtain new opportunities for readjustment and sanctification, but will also endorse our promises and aspirations before Jesus regarding the Higher Life.

~ 113 ~

Your Faith

Then he said to her, "Daughter, be of good cheer; your faith has saved you; go in peace." – Jesus (Lk. 8:48)

It is important to notice that, after having dispensed beneficial assistance, the Divine Master always referred to the wonder of faith, the sublime heritage of those who seek him.

On many occasions, we hear his expressive affirmation, "Your faith has saved you." After experiencing relief or healing, the infirm in body and soul hear that generous pronouncement. This is because human will and trust are powerful factors in the development and illumination of life.

Navigators who have no route to follow and who have nothing to trust in will only reach port because random forces are on their side; they are completely unaware of what might happen to them.

Patients who are skeptical about the effectiveness of all medications are the first to work against their own wellbeing.

Those who are disenchanted with everything do not expect anything to be useful.

Empty souls clamor in vain for the share of happiness they think the world owes them. The state of denial in which they wander transforms their lives into deadened zones that resemble electric insulators: the life-giving current may pass through them, but they remain insensitive.

Amid the enterprises and needs of your pathway, do not insulate yourself in negativity. Jesus can overcome anything, and your true friends will do everything possible for you; however, neither the Master nor your friends can provide you fully with the happiness you seek without the aid of your faith, because you are also a child of the same God and have the same potential for spiritual growth.

~ 114 ~

The New Athenians

But when they heard about the resurrection of the dead, some scoffed; but others said, "We will hear you again regarding this matter." (Acts 17:32)

Paul's contact with the Athenians on the Areopagus represents a very interesting lesson for new disciples.

As long as the Apostle was commenting on his impressions of the famous city – perhaps stoking his listeners' vanity by referring to their sanctuaries and subtly playing upon their reasoning – they listened attentively. It is possible that they would have praised him fervently if he had stuck to his initial philosophical viewpoint. Athens would have revered him as a wise man, presenting him to the world in the special mold of its unforgettable figures.

Paul, however, went on to refer to the resurrection of the dead, giving them a glimpse of the glorious continuation of life beyond the trifles of earth. And from that moment on, the audience started to feel uncomfortable and scoffed at his loving and sincere words. In the end, they left him practically alone.

This example fits in perfectly with what happens nowadays. Within the various areas of modern culture, numerous workers for Christ are listened to attentively and are respected by the authorities on the subjects of their specialty. But when they openly declare their belief in a life beyond the physical body, as they affirm the law of responsibility beyond the grave, they immediately receive scoffing laughter from the admirers of a minute before, who leave them at once with the impression of a veritable desert.

~ 115 ~

The Gate

So Jesus said again: "Truly I say unto you, I am the gate for the sheep." (Jn. 10:7)

It is not enough to embody the gentleness and tenderness of a sheep in order to reach the Divine Kingdom.

The sheep must recognize the gate of redemption with the necessary discernment, and they must watch their step and disregard the appeals of an inferior order that appear by the wayside.

From this we can conclude that, in order to be victorious, prudence must be combined with caution regarding the direction to follow.

The loss of a flock does not always result from an animal attack, but because the sheep have wandered carelessly beyond natural barriers in search of their own pasture, deaf to the shepherd's voice or blind to the protective gate. How many sheep are attacked unexpectedly by the dreadful wolf because they are fascinated by neighboring green pastures and wander off their own path, breaking down fences in answer to destructive impulses?

This is what happens to people in the course of their lives.

How many noble spirits have lost precious opportunities due to their own imprudence? Even though they possess admirable qualities, they sometimes become arbitrary and capricious. In the majority of cases, they are like virtuous and useful sheep, who, after acquiring a number of ennobling traits, forget the gate they are supposed to reach and break the necessary and beneficial discipline in order to hand themselves over to the devouring wolf.

~ 116 ~

Listen to Them

Abraham replied, "They have Moses and the Prophets; let them listen to them." (Lk. 16:29)

Abraham's response to the rich man in the parable is still a valuable lesson for our daily life on the common path.

Innumerable people approach the fountains of spiritual revelation, but they do not break free of their selfish ties in a way that enables them to see and hear what is in their best interests.

Exactly one century ago[1] a more intense interchange was established between the two planes in the great movement of revivified Christianity; nonetheless, there are disciples who look up at heaven in dismay because they have never received a direct message from a father or son who shared in their human experience. Some go so far as to turn away from the path because of this. For them, the phenomena and revelations of

[1] This was written in 1950 and refers to the publication in 1857 of *The Spirits' Book* by Allan Kardec, which contains the basis for the Spiritist Doctrine and its teachings. – Tr.

evangelical Spiritism are merely a set of untruths, because they never received anything from *dead family members* during their many years of observation.

This is nonsense, however.

Who can guarantee the perpetuity of the fragile links of terrestrial connections?

The animal impulse has its limits.

Let no one justify their spiritual blindness on account of a personal unfulfilled desire.

The world has received its full share of messages and emissaries for thousands of years. The big issue, however, has not lain in demanding the truth in order to attend to the exclusive circle of each person, but rather in having each individual decide as how to proceed with his or her own qualities regarding the eternal realities.

~ 117 ~

In the Family

Learn first of all to be caring toward your own family and to repay your parents, for this is pleasing to God. – Paul (1 Tim. 5:4)

The family struggle is a fundamental problem in human redemption. How can we be benefactors for a hundred or a thousand people if we have not yet learned to serve five or ten? This is a logical question that applies to all sincere disciples of Christianity.

Good preacher and bad servant are two titles that do not go together.

The Apostle recommends being caring amid household activities; however, he is not referring to the caring that weeps without courage when faced with afflictive challenges, but the caring that recognizes problematic areas in the home and strives to eliminate them, awaiting the divine determination at the right time.

We know of many brothers and sisters who feel spiritually lonely amongst persons connected to their personal group through blood ties, and who, as a result, become very discouraged.

It is crucial, however, to examine these temporary corporeal bonds and realize that there are no casual unions in the family household, a place where, for the time being, saving and regenerating trials prevail. Thus, no one should disdain this sacred opportunity of service, even if overwhelmed by incomprehension. It would be a grave wrong to overlook the infinite possibilities of this illuminating endeavor.

We cannot possibly help the whole world if we cannot be useful in the little home where the Father's will has temporarily placed us.

Before making a great personal contribution to worldwide service, disciples should learn to work on behalf of their family members right now, knowing that such an effort represents an essential achievement.

~ 118 ~

For this Reason

Not repaying evil with evil or insult with insult, but with blessing, for that is the purpose for which you have been called. (1 Pet. 3:9)

The ranks of complainers have always been numerous in every effort for the good.

In the evangelical apostolate, we see this general rule at work as well.

In obedience to this harmful habit, many disciples prefer the path of strife or of scandalous dissent. However, a little reasoning would awaken the community of disciples to a greater comprehension.

Would Jesus ask us to get involved in useless conflicts only to repeat situations of individual caprice or tyrannical conduct? If this were the case, the ministry of the Kingdom would be entrusted to the obstinate, the arguers or to the physically strong.

It is nonsense for the servant of the Good News to yield to baseless complaining.

What are bitterness, persecution, slander, brutality and misunderstanding, after all? They are age-old characteristics that torment souls on earth. The Lord has called us into his ranks in order to help wipe these characteristics out. Do not foster them by making room for them.

The Christian is a living point of resistance to evil wherever he or she is.

Think about this and seek to understand the meaning of the verb "to bear."

Do not forget your obligation to serve with Jesus.

It is for this reason that we have been called.

~ 119 ~

Always Be of Assistance

But Paul answered: "Why are you weeping and breaking my heart?" (Acts 21:13)

One of the most dramatic passages in the *Acts of the Apostles* describes Paul of Tarsus' preparation to face the testimony that awaited him in Jerusalem.

There is not a shadow of hesitation in the heroic soul of this fighter. As usual, his spirit is ready. But his companions are weeping and lamenting, eliciting a painful question that flows from the sensitive and valiant heart of this warrior of the Gospel.

In spite of his indomitable, serene energy, Paul felt the lack of friends as courageous as himself.

His travel companions were sincerely ready for death; however, they did not know how to express the sentiments of a faithful soul. Weeping and lamenting never helps in moments of difficult testimony. Whoever weeps beside a friend in a precarious position undermines his or her endurance.

Jesus wept in the Garden of Gethsemane when he was alone, but in Jerusalem, under the weight of the cross, he tells the kind women who were supporting him to stop their anguished tears. On the morning of the Resurrection, he asks Magdalene to explain the reason for her tears at the tomb.

This lesson is of great significance for all disciples.

If a loved one has endured a necessary affliction for a long time, do not fall into useless desperation. Complaining solves nothing. Instead of embittering him or her with your tears, reach out.

~ 120 ~

Reconciliation

"Reconcile quickly with your adversary while you are on the way with him so that he does not hand you over to the judge, and so that the judge does not hand you over to the officer, and so that you will not be thrown into prison." – Jesus (Mt. 5:25)

After having received the exhortation of this passage, many ennobled souls suffer inwardly when confronted with the hardness of a former adversary who is unwilling to reconcile.

The Master's warning, however, is fundamentally consoling to the individual conscience.

The Master's recommendation to "Reconcile" is like saying "Do your part."

Correct your past errors as much as possible; make every effort to display your persevering goodwill. Insist on kindness and understanding.

If your adversary is unmoved, think of the time when you too were unaware of your fundamental obligations and see if you yourself did not act even worse. If he or she is a bad person, count him or her among the sick and imbalanced on the road to recovery.

Do as much good as possible while you are walking the same path, because if your enemy is so implacable that he or she seeks to turn you over to the judge at any cost, you too will have evidence and proofs to present. A legitimate trial includes all the pieces, and only spirits thoroughly impenetrable to the good will suffer the rigors of justice to the extreme.

Strive therefore as much as possible for harmony, but if your adversary scorns your good intentions, reconcile yourself with your own conscience and wait trustingly.

~ 121 ~

The Manure Pile

"It is fit for neither the soil nor the manure pile; it is thrown out. He who has ears to hear, let him hear." – Jesus (Lk. 14:35)

According to what we can tell, Jesus lent significant meaning to the manure pile.

Soil and compost are given essential importance in this passage. With the former, we do the sowing; with the latter, it is possible to apply fertilizers where needed.

By imitating the attitude of the Pharisees of old, a large number of disciples flee at their first encounter with their neighbor's "manure zones"; however, this is because they are unaware of their useful purposes.

The Gospel is full of lessons in this area of illuminative knowledge.

If Joseph of Galilee or Mary of Nazareth symbolize soils full of virtue, the same cannot be said of the disciples who, at every step, must resort to the stream of tears that stream down from the manure pile of human remorse and weakness in order to fertilize the impoverished soil of their hearts. For example, how much fertilizer of this nature did Magdalene and Paul need before they achieved the glorious positions for which they are known?

Let us transform our miseries into lessons.

Let us identify the manure we have piled up around ourselves out of our own ignorance and change it into fertilizer for our "inner soil"; in doing so, we will find the right solution to our greatest ills.

~ 122 ~

Sin and Sinner

Beloved, do not follow evil, but the good. The one who does good is of God, but the one who does evil has not seen God. (3 Jn. 11)

Human society should not divide itself into camps where the good are on one side and the evil on the other. Instead, it should live as a huge family that includes spirits that have begun to understand the Father and spirits that have not yet managed to sense him.

Of course, for many years to come the words "evil" and "wickedness" will continue to appear in dictionaries, defining certain mental attitudes of a low order; however, one must agree that the question of evil has been receiving new interpretations in human knowledge.

The Evangelist gives us the correct idea about evil. John does not say that wicked individuals have been exiled from our Father or that they are kept apart from Creation. John merely affirms that they "have not seen God."

This does not mean that we should just fold our arms before the poisonous weeds and pestilent areas on the path; however, it does oblige us to remember that the farmer does not pull thorn bushes and refuse from the soil in order to leave it full of holes.

Many believe that "fallen men and women" should be done away with forever. But Jesus did not look at it like that. Whenever he lovingly addressed the sinner, he knew that, before anything else, he was facing an unwell, unhappy person, from whom the distinguishing marks of eternity could not be taken.

Fight crime, but help the individual who has become entangled in its dark web.

The Master pointed out the constant battle against evil, but he awaits true fraternity among humans as the sublime milestone of the Heavenly Kingdom.

~ 123 ~

The Common Condition

Immediately the boy's father exclaimed in tears, "I believe, Lord; help my unbelief." (Mk. 9:24)

This man from the crowd, who brought his sick child to Jesus, is a characteristic image of the common spirit of humankind.

Religious circles comment a great deal on faith in God; however, during stormy moments there are few devotees who remain firm in their trust.

The masses give a lot of attention to outward worship ceremonies and they take part in the religious teachings related to their faith; however, when faced with offence, nearly all of them slide down the cliff of mutual accusations.

If a missionary fails, disbandment follows. The community of believers keeps its eyes on fallible men and women, blind to purposes or indifferent to institutions. In a climate of such spiritual insecurity, people believe and disbelieve, trusting today but collapsing tomorrow.

We are still faced with the ambiguity of immature spirits that have barely begun to understand what responsibility is.

Therefore, happy are they who, like the father in need, come to Christ confessing their precarious inner conviction. Thus, as they affirm their faith verbally, they will at the same time be pleading for help for their lack of faith, attesting with tears to their own miserable condition.

~ 124 ~

There Is No Lack

"But if I let them go home hungry, they will faint on the way because some of them have come from far away." – Jesus (Mk. 8:3)

Jesus' concern for the multitude has remained alive throughout time.

How many religious institutions beat within the hearts of nations at the influx of providential love from the Divine Master?

There may be wicked, desperate individuals who persevere in evil and denial, but there is no society that lacks the help of faith. Of course, even primitive societies receive assistance from the Lord in accordance with the rusticity of their primitive understanding. There is no lack of nourishment from heaven for God's creatures. If some spirits declare their disbelief in God's fatherhood, it is because they are either incapable or sick after having given in to inner ruin.

Jesus manifests his untiring concern by nurturing the souls of his wards in a thousand different ways, from the hut of the native to the cathedrals of the great cities.

In these places of sublime assistance, men and women gradually learn to nourish themselves spiritually until they bring the place of worship into their homes, and then from the domestic sanctuary into the corners of their own hearts.

Few people ponder the infinite mercy that is served at the edifying table of religious ideas.

The Master bows to the good of all people. Filled with love and self-sacrifice, he knows how to use specific resources to nourish the ignorant and the wise, the believer and the questioner, the rebel and the wretch. Better than anyone else, Jesus understands that if this were not so, people would fall exhausted into the deep precipices that border the evolutionary path.

~ 125 ~

Separation

"But I tell you the truth: It is for your own good that I go away." – Jesus (Jn. 16:7)

This statement by the Master resounds within our innermost fibers.

No one knew how to love as much as he did, yet he was the first to realize that it was fitting for him to leave for the good of his companions.

What would have happened if Jesus had insisted on remaining?

Most likely, the multitudes of earth would have accentuated and consolidated their selfish inclinations.

Because the Divine Friend went to Lazarus in the tomb, people would no longer resign themselves to separation because of death. For having cleansed a few lepers, no one in the future would accept the beneficial help of physical diseases. The logical result would have been a widespread disturbance in the evolutionary mechanism.

The Master needed to go away so that the personal effort of each individual would be made visible in the divine plan for the world. Otherwise, the indolence of some and the selfishness of others would have continued.

Under different characteristics, this important time for the evangelical family is repeated every day in our kinship clusters.

How often do widowhood, orphanhood, the suffering from being apart, perplexity and pain arise to serve the high purpose of the common good?

Recall the above passage from the Gospel whenever separation makes you weep, for if the death of the physical body means renewal for those who go away, it is also new life for those who remain behind.

~ 126 ~

The Thorn

And so that I would not become haughty because of these exceedingly great revelations, I was given a thorn in my flesh, a messenger of Satan. – Paul (2 Cor. 12:7)

Self-praise is a highly dangerous attitude for people who supposedly are unaware of the fact that they are in a realm of arduous service, where they must bear difficult witness each and every day. This mental attitude is not only alarming but erroneous, because there will come a time when the thorn in the heart will unexpectedly appear.

Prudent disciples will nourish confidence without boasting, and will show themselves to be courageous without being presumptuous. They recognize the extent of the debt they owe the Master and they do not glorify themselves, knowing that all glory belongs to the Lord.

There are a lot of unwatchful and troubled people who, after having received the adulation of the multitudes, proceed to suffer the bitterness of loneliness. Many of them take great pleasure in the heights of fame, as if they had become indestructible idols, only to weep alone later on with the thorn they had ignored in the depths of their soul.

Why pretend to be infallible teachers when we are but simple learners?

Would it not be better to serve the Lord with prudence in youth or old age, in abundance or scarcity, as a manager or subordinate, observing our vulnerable points in the shortcomings and imperfection of what we have been up till now?

Let us remember that Paul of Tarsus met Jesus personally; he was appointed for divine service in Antioch by the very voices of heaven; he fought, worked and suffered for the Gospel of the Kingdom, and in writing to the Corinthians, already old and tired, he still referred to the thorn he had been given so that he would not be haughty as he carried out the sublime work of revelation.

~ 127 ~

The Law of Return

"And those who have done good will go to the resurrection of life; those who have done evil to the resurrection of condemnation." – Jesus (Jn. 5:29)

In few passages of the Gospel is the law of reincarnation implied as clearly as in this one, where the Master's teaching refers to the resurrection of condemnation.

How would theologians interested in the existence of a burning and eternal hell understand these words?

Individuals dedicated to the good will find the fountain of life as they bathe in the waters of corporeal death. Their accomplishments of the future follow their upward path in direct correspondence with the persevering efforts they exerted while on the path of sanctifying spirituality, whereas those who have taken pleasure in evil annul their own possibilities of resurrection in the light.

They must repeat their expiatory course.

It is the return to the lesson or to the remedy.

There is no other alternative.

The law of return, therefore, is amply contained in Jesus' synthesis.

Resurrection means rebirth. The meaning of renewal cannot be harmonized with the theory of eternal punishment.

In final and absolute verdicts there is no saving recourse. According to what the Master is saying here, however, we can see that Divine Providence is much richer and magnanimous than one might think.

There will be a resurrection for all, but with the difference that the righteous will have it in a new life, and the evil in a new condemnation as a consequence of their own wrongdoing.

~ 128 ~

Because They Do Not Know

"You will be the target of such things because they have known neither the Father nor me."
– Jesus (Jn. 16:3)

Painful perplexities quite often assail disciples, leading them to ask why.

Why is there disharmony surrounding the fraternal effort?

The journey towards the good encounters dark obstacles.

One tries to abide by the light, but the darkness enters the path. One formulates simple plans for charity, but ill-will tries to disrupt it at the first attempt to implement it.

Nearly always, this destructive demonstration originates from individuals distinguished by their prominent position, appointed by the force of circumstances to carry out the function of guiding public opinion. In most instances, they are the ones who set themselves up as expositors of improper impositions and demands.

However, the sincere disciple of Jesus should not waste time on unjustifiable questions and anxieties.

The Divine Master clarified this great problem in advance.

Ignorance is the common source of imbalance. If this or that group of individuals tries to impede manifestations of the good, it is because they do not yet know the blessings of heaven.

Nothing more than that.

It is essential, therefore, for each disciple to disregard the darkness that still dominates most of the earth and live in the light that vibrates in service to the Lord.

~ 129 ~

When He Broke the Bread

Then they told them what had happened to them on the way, and how he was recognized by them when he broke the bread. (Lk. 24:35)

The occasion on which the Master is recognized by the grieving disciples on their way to Emmaus is of great importance.

Jesus had accompanied them like a nameless friend, setting the truth in their hearts with caring, tender explanations.

For most of the way they were in the company of this wise, loving man, whom they considered to be a generous and affable stranger. It was only when he broke the bread that they recognized their beloved Master.

These two disciples had not been able to identify him by his words or his warm gestures; nevertheless, as soon as the materialized bread appeared, all their doubts vanished and they believed.

Has not the same been occurring for millennia?

Multitudes of aspirants to the faith have given up their divine work because, after certain expectations, they were unable to attain the advantages they were hoping for in the realm of human struggle. With no financial guarantee or fulfilled whims, they fail to partake of a faith that is renewing, upright and trustworthy.

It is necessary to strive against such shortsightedness of the soul.

May the Lord be praised for all the lessons and testimonies he confers upon us; however, you will be far from the truth if you seek him solely in the "breaking" of fragmentary and perishable material things.

~130~

Where Are They?

"Take my yoke upon you and learn from me, for I am gentle and humble in heart, and you will find rest for your souls." – Jesus (Mt. 11:29)

Jesus directed his attention to the afflicted and disheartened multitude, proclaiming his divine aim to give them relief.

"Come unto me!" invited the Master. "Take my yoke upon you and learn from me, for I am gentle and humble in heart!"

His loving plea has resounded throughout the centuries of Christianity.

The multitude of the desperate and the oppressed of the earth is enormous in spite of his loving invitation.

In the words "Come unto me!" the Master hopes, of course, that sad and anxious souls will seek him in order to acquire divine teaching. However, not all the afflicted intend to renounce the object of their despair, nor do all the sad desire to flee the darkness to find the light.

The majority of the disheartened even try to satisfy their wretched desires with Jesus' protection by uttering peculiar prayers.

However, when sufferers sincerely direct their thoughts to Christ, they can hear him in the silence of their inner sanctuary, encouraging their spirit to scorn the reproachable arguments of their lower nature.

Where are the afflicted of the earth who would want to exchange their slavery to their personal passions for the gentle yoke of Jesus Christ?

The holy words "Come unto me!" were spoken to them. The Gospel holds a powerful light for the renewal they need so much.

~ 131 ~

The World and Faith

"Let the Christ, the King of Israel, come down from the cross so that we may see and believe." (Mk. 15:32)

Because there are very few people capable of truly understanding pure faith in its essential character, we meet those who have offended Christ in order to confirm him.

The miracle mentality has always swum on the surface of the senses without reaching the realm of the eternal spirit, and if it does not achieve its unworthy purposes, it degenerates into scornful challenges.

In the case of the Master, these remarks do not stem solely from the mob. Mark states that the chief priests and scribes also took part in insulting Jesus, as if to say that intellectuality does not imply spiritual development.

The offenders remained deaf to the Good News of the Kingdom, blind to the benefits they received and insensitive to the loving touch that Jesus had directed to all hearts.

They were only looking for a spectacle.

If Christ would come down from the cross as if by magic, all the problems of their inferior belief would have been resolved.

However, Jesus gave them no other response than silence, giving them to understand that the magnitude of his gesture was inaccessible to their childish purposes.

If you are a sincere disciple of the Gospel, do not forget that even today the situation is not much different.

Work consciously in the service of faith.

Unite with the Lord; give all you can in his name and continue working to extend the good, knowing that the vast unevolved world will only ask you maliciously for distractions and signs.

~ 132 ~

In All Things

We commend ourselves in all things: in much patience, in afflictions, in hardships, in distresses. – Paul (2 Cor. 6:4)

Most adherents of the Gospel do not seriously consider the religious aspect of life except in outward worship activities. Many believe that it is enough for them to assiduously attend gatherings of the faithful, and all the enigmas of the soul, as far as our relationship with God is concerned, will be deciphered.

However, the teachings of Christ call for individual renewal and growth in all circumstances.

What can be said of people who are apparently contrite during public acts of their religious creed but who use profanity in the sanctuary of their home? There are many who say they are believers while amongst the crowd, but who show themselves to be lazy at work, fraught in their suffering, unrestrained in happiness, unfaithful in their doings, and blasphemous in the troubles of the heart.

Would Jesus strive for the development of his followers only to be praised by them while they kneel a few hours per week? To attribute such a purpose to the Master would be to demean his sublime principles.

It is crucial that disciples make themselves commendable in all things, demonstrating the excellence of the ideas that nourish them both at home and at church, in their daily activities and in the public streets.

Of course, no one has to live solely with their hands folded or gazing into the heavens; however, let us not forget that gentleness, goodwill, cooperation and politeness are divine aspects of the living prayer of a disciple of Christ.

~ 133 ~

The Great Future

"But for now, my kingdom is not of this world." – Jesus (Jn. 18:36)

Since the early days of Christianity, we have seen disciples who have deliberately withdrawn from the world, alleging that the Kingdom of the Lord is not to be found on earth.

They kneel for long periods of time in houses of worship, and they believe that in such an escape they achieve sanctity.

Many cross their arms in front of works of regeneration, and when asked why, they express repulsion at the disagreeable pictures the earthly experience offers them, stating that Christ told Pilate that his Kingdom had not yet been established in the circles of the human struggle.

However, one must remember that Christ did not disinherit the planet. His word did not warrant the complete denial of heavenly happiness for the earth, but only defined the environment at that time without disregarding hope for the future.

The Master, clarified: "But for now, my Kingdom is not of this world."

This statement reveals his confidence.

Jesus, therefore, cannot endorse the erroneous attitude of workers who have become discouraged simply because the darkness has become thicker around temporary problems, or because human wounds at times become more painful. Such circumstances are often subject to pure visual illusion.

Divine activity never ceases, and it is precisely in the arena of beneficial struggle that disciples will carve out their victories.

Thus, we should not desert the world for the contemplative posture, but instead we are to press on confidently toward the great future.

~ 134 ~

Spiritual Nutrition

It is good for the heart to be strengthened by grace instead of dainties, which are of no value to anyone who indulges in them. – Paul (Heb. 13:9)

There are nutritional vices of the soul, just as there are nutritional vices of the body.

Many people trade pure water for stimulating beverages, just as many people prefer pernicious illusion when dealing with spiritual problems.

In order to be effective for the eternal life, nourishment for the heart has to be based on the simple realities of the evolutionary path.

It is crucial for us to strengthen ourselves with illuminative principles, without heeding the dazzling fantasies that come from the outside. And it is precisely on the religious path that such effort demands broader refinement.

Generally speaking, believers are always eager for situations that can satisfy their pernicious whims, just like a gourmet yearns for exotic dishes. However, just as delights of the table are not necessary for fundamental activities, the thrilling sensations of spirit phenomena are useless to the soul if it does not possess sufficient inner resources to understand their purpose. Many disciples regard their religious experience as a purely intellectual matter. But it is crucial to realize that, in order to be definitely incorporated, the nourishment of the soul requires a heart that is sincerely interested in the divine truths. When individuals assume this inner attitude, they truly strengthen themselves for sublimation. They realize that there is such an abundance of useful work material around them that they place any temporary sensation on the lowest rungs of the evolutionary ladder.

~ 135 ~

Necessary Renewal

Do not quench the spirit. – Paul (1 Thes. 5:19)

When the Apostle to the Gentiles wrote this exhortation, he did not mean that the spirit could be destroyed. Instead, he was trying to renew the mental attitude of those who were suffocating their higher spiritual tendencies.

We often see people who go against their own conscience in order to avoid being labeled as spiritual. Nevertheless, incarnate souls are placed in the laborious learning experience in order to rise from the world as glorified spirits. This is the highest purpose of the human school.

However, humans are still a long way from the great truth. They habitually prefer strict conventionalism, and only at much cost do they open their understanding to the realities of the soul. Actually, customs are powerful determining elements in the evolutionary process, but only when inspired by principles of a higher order.

Therefore, we must not suffocate the seeds of the spiritually constructive life that sprout daily in our hearts under the influence of the Merciful Father.

There are brothers and sisters who leave the earth through the same door of ignorance and indifference that they entered it. Thus, as disciples look back on the activities of each day, they should ask themselves: What have I accomplished? Have I accentuated the traits of the inferior individual of yesterday, or have I developed the lofty spiritual qualities that I want to retain tomorrow?

~ 136 ~

Conflict

So I find this law within me: whenever I want to do good, evil is with me. – Paul (Rom. 7:21)

Sincere disciples of the Gospel, such as Paul of Tarsus, encounter enormous conflict in their own nature.

Almost always, they are confronted by huge problems as they bear witness. At the exact moment where they should express the presence of the Divine Companion in their heart, one word or one fleeting attitude betrays them to their own conscience, indicating the persistence of old weaknesses.

Most experience feelings of shame and sorrow.

Some attribute these downfalls to the influence of evil spirits and usually seek the enemy outside themselves, whereas they should cleanse their inner selves of the undesirable cause of their attunement to evil.

There can be no doubt that we are still at a stage that is far removed from where we can live free from adverse vibrations; however, we must verify within ourselves the truth of Paul's observation.

As long as people remain in cold indifference or restless obstinacy, they are not called to make a pure analysis; however, as soon as they awaken to spiritual renewal, their inner camp becomes a battlefield.

Against the flickering aspiration of the good today rises the heavy baggage of darkness that we have accumulated over the centuries in our soul. Therefore, much serenity and endurance is indispensable on our part so that the progress we have made is not lost.

The Lord grants us the clarity of today so that we may forget the darkness of yesterday, thus preparing us for tomorrow as we make our way toward the imperishable light.

~ 137 ~

Enemies

"Therefore, love your enemies." – Jesus (Lk. 6:35)

This affirmation by the Divine Master deserves close consideration everywhere. Of course, this recommendation to love our enemies requires a special analysis.

Generally speaking, the masses attribute the verb "to love" only to activities of affection. In order to demonstrate love in worldly terms, people have to use a lot of words and tender attitudes, even though we know that love can shine in a person's heart without any superficial outward display. Although the Father confers on us wearisome and difficult lives on the earth or other worlds, we cannot attribute to him any denial of love.

Regarding the Divine Friend's statement, we must think long and hard about it.

Where there is strife, there is antagonism, revealing the existence of circumstances where agreement would not be right if the common good is at stake. When the Master counseled us to love our enemies, he was not suggesting that we go along with those who deliberately steal or destroy, nor was he ordering us to increase the wings of perversity or malicious intent. What he was really suggesting is that we help the cruelest individuals, not with undue approval but with the sincere and fraternal intention of helping them return to the divine path through patience, reconstructive recourse or restorative endeavors. More than anything else, the Master was concerned with protecting us against the poison of hatred and keeping us from falling into petty, useless or disastrous arguments.

Therefore, love those who show that they are in conflict with your heart. Support them fraternally with all the possibilities of assistance within your reach, convinced that such a measure will free you from the calamitous duel of evil against evil.

~ 138 ~

Let Us Heed This

For Christ sent me not to baptize but to preach the Gospel; not in the wisdom of words, lest the cross of Christ have been in vain. – Paul (1 Cor. 1:17)

Generally speaking, while we are incarnate, we feel a vain pleasure in attracting as many people as possible to our way of thinking.

Invariably, we are good preachers and are eminently deft at coming up with reasoning that overwhelms the points of view of those who cannot understand us in the current circumstances of the struggle.

At our first small triumph, we get busy consulting the holy books, not to acquire more enlightenment, but with the objective of investigating the human letters of the divine scriptures, seeking to point out the weak arguments of our opponents.

If we are Roman Catholics, we insist on our friends going to mass and receiving the physical sacraments; if we are adherents of the reformed churches, we expect them to participate in the worship service; and if we are Spiritists, we seek to increase their number of sessions of communication with the invisible plane.

Such efforts may be praiseworthy in some aspects; however, it is imperative to remember that students of the Gospel, who sincerely try to understand the Christ, feel highly renewed regarding their inner conduct.

When Jesus enters people's hearts, he changes them into living witnesses of the good, and he instructs them to preach the Gospel to their brothers and sisters with the example of their own lives. Once they comprehend Jesus, they do not stop purely and simply with impressive words; they live in accordance with the Master, exemplifying the work and the love that illumine life so that the glory of the cross will not have been in vain.

~ 139 ~

Offerings

For he did this once, offering himself. – Paul (Heb. 7:27)

Human beings always do well in an affluent home under a blue sky. However, as soon as problems appear, they immediately look for someone to replace them in the places of annoyance and pain. They often pay a heavy price for this escape, indefinitely postponing the beneficial experience to which they were invited by the hand of the Lord.

In light of this, religious leaders down through time have created complicated problems for the offerings of faith.

In primitive rituals, there was no hesitation in sacrificing the young and children.

Over the course of time, people resorted to sacrificing sheep, bulls and goats in their sanctuaries.

For many centuries, offerings consisted of riches and valuable objects meant for worship services.

With all these demonstrations, however, people were seeking nothing but to attract exclusive favoritism from God, as if the Father were actually inclined towards these earthly particularities.

The majority of those who render material offerings in houses of worship are not moved to do so out of love for the divine work; their deliberate purpose is to buy heaven's grace, thus exempting themselves from working on their self-betterment.

Regarding this matter, however, Christ has provided a most precious answer to his wards in the world. Far from pleading any prerogatives, he sent no substitutes to Calvary or animals to be sacrificed in temples; instead, he personally embraced the heavy cross to sacrifice himself on behalf of all, thereby demonstrating that all disciples will be compelled to offer their own personal testimony on the altar of their own lives.

~ 140 ~

Let Us Know How to Remember

Remember my chains. – Paul (Col. 4:18)

In their customary immaturity and rashness, believers remember only the luminous aura of the spirits sanctified on earth.

Many imagine that it will be easy to find them beyond the grave in order to listen to their cherished remembrances.

They expect heaven to be only a bright, shining resting place in the immensity of the cosmos…

How many will only remember Paul in his glorification? In this remark to the Colossians, however, the great Apostle exhorts his friends to remember his chains, as if to say that disciples should not set their thoughts on the anticipation of heavenly ease, but rather that they should seriously think about the work that is required to receive the Divine Kingdom.

The attainment of sublimated spirituality also has its pathways, and one must travel them.

Before setting our sights on the resplendent crown of the faithful Apostles, let us meditate on the thorns that wounded their brow.

Paul was able to reach such heights, but as he scaled the mountain, how many blows from whips, stones and scorn he had to bear as he adapted to the teachings of the Christ!

Do not set your eyes only on the manifested superiority of those you admire and respect. Remember to imitate them by valuing the sacrificial work to which they devoted themselves to reach the divine goal.

~ 141 ~

Fraternal Love

Let fraternal love remain. – Paul (Heb. 13:1)

Family affections, blood ties and natural affinities can be very holy manifestations of the soul when individuals raise them to the altar of the higher sentiments; however, the spirit should not fall under the weight of its personal inclinations.

Equilibrium is the ideal position.

By being overly protective, countless parents cause their children harm.

Due to excessive worry, many married couples descend to the caverns of despair, confronted by the insatiable monsters of jealousy that destroys their happiness.

Because of carelessness, beautiful friendships end in the abyss of darkness.

The above evangelical appeal, therefore, is of great importance.

Pure fraternity is the most sublime of the relationships between souls.

People who believe they are children of God and sincere brothers and sisters of humankind are not victims of the ghosts of spite, envy, ambition or mistrust. Those who love one another fraternally are elated with the joy of others and they are pleased with the good fortune that visits their neighbor.

The tumultuous affections that are common on the earth pass volcanically and uselessly.

In the web of reincarnation, affections change constantly. Sublime and pure fraternal love, representing the supreme objective of people's understanding, is the imperishable light that will survive on the eternal path.

~ 142 ~

Reprisals

The fact that you are suing one another means you have already committed a wrong. Why not endure an injustice? Why not endure harm? – Paul (1 Cor. 6:7)

Contentions are not always limited to the courts of justice in the scandalous arena of public lawsuits.

They appear on a greater scale in homes and institutions. There, they arise from mental disorderliness and surreptitious conversation in the unseen muck of hatred that asphyxiates hearts and saps their strength. If they do exist, however, it is because members of the family or the organization feed them with the oil of repressed animosity.

Many disciples become victims of such troubles because they take refuge in erroneous regenerative principles.

Usually, a large number display an aggressive attitude with sword in hand, dueling heatedly in the illusory belief of setting their neighbor straight.

Ready to protest, to accuse, to criticize loudly, they explain that they are serving the truth. But why do they not express their faith by heroically enduring injustice and harm in the silence of a faithful soul rather than opting for reprisal?

How many homes would be happier, how many institutions would become permanent fountainheads of light if believers in the Gospel would learn to keep quiet in order to speak advantageously at the proper time?

We are not referring to ordinary individuals, but rather to disciples of Jesus.

How much the world will profit when followers of Christ feel fortunate for being simple instruments of the good in the Divine Hands, forgetting the old objective of being the arbitrary directors of the Work of Heaven?

~ 143 ~

Do Not Tyrannize

With many such parables he spoke the word to them according to what they could understand. (Mk. 4:33)

Every now and then, we encounter preachers who are strict and demanding in the dissemination of the evangelical teachings.

Such an anomaly is not seen only in the general aspect of preaching per se. In personal circles, it is common to see stern and zealous individuals desperately demanding their friends and acquaintances to espouse the religious principles that they themselves have embraced.

Heated arguments ensue, promoting poisonous bitterness.

Beautiful expressions of love are shaken at their foundation by unwarranted offences.

However, if disciples are truly imbued with the purpose of union with the Master, this attitude can be easily corrected.

The Lord taught those who listened only "according to what they could understand."

To the Apostles he conveyed teachings of a lofty symbolic quality, whereas to the multitudes he transmitted fundamental truths by way of simple stories. His speech varied according to the spiritual needs of those who gathered around him. He never violated anyone's natural position.

If you are in the Lord's service, consider the imperatives of illumination, for the world needs Christian servants, not doctrinal tyrants.

~ 144 ~

Make Preparations

"Then he will show you a large furnished upper room. Make preparations there." – Jesus (Lk. 22:12).

That furnished upper room to which Jesus was referring is a perfect symbol of the internal dwelling of the soul.

In looking at nature, which offers priceless lessons in every area of activity, we can see that people wait for each new day to renew activity in their home. Here, they sweep up the dirt; there, they decorate the walls. The furniture, almost always the same, goes through the daily cleaning process.

Conscientious individuals will realize that most of the actions in their physical experience are geared toward incessantly preparing themselves for the life they will face after the death of the body.

If this is the case with the material aspect of earthly life, what may be said about spiritual efforts for the eternal path?

Of course, countless people go through each day unconsciously, almost mechanically. They get out of bed, feed the perishable body, spend all their time on trifles, and then go to sleep again each night.

Sincere disciples, however, know that they have reached the symbolic upper room of the heart. Although they cannot change their ideas every day – just like the furniture in their home – they give them a new shine at every moment by sublimating their impulses, renewing their concepts, elevating their desires, and continually improving the laudable qualities they already possess.

Merely earthly-minded people keep themselves in the expectation of an organic death; spiritual people await the Divine Master in order to consolidate their redemption.

Therefore, do not abandon the upper room of faith, and within it make continuous preparations.

~ 145 ~

Workers

Seek to present yourself to God as an approved worker who does not need to be ashamed. – Paul (2 Tim. 2:15)

Since time immemorial, people have thought of a thousand ways in which to present themselves to God and his messengers.

Many worry an entire lifetime about how to ready their clothes for the heavenly concert, while countless believers carefully annotate their grievances in order to recite them as a long list of complaints to the Lord in hopes of distinction in the future world.

Most devotees would like to begin their journey after death as saints; however, there is no better way to ponder what our true position is than where we find ourselves as workers.

The world is a department of the Divine Workplace.

Professorships and hoes are not elements of humiliating division, but rather hierarchical steps for different coworkers.

The edifying path unfolds before everyone.

Here, holes are opened up in the productive soil; there, books are used for the furrows of intelligence, but the spirit is the living foundation of the service expressed either way.

Workers fall into different categories, but there is only one field.

In reality, therefore, no one should be concerned about fancy titles, because there is a lot of work to do in every sector of dignifying activity, and the result is always the fruit of well-performed cooperation. For this reason, we conclude with Paul that the greatest victory of disciples is to be able to present themselves to the Lord some day as approved workers.

~ 146 ~

Following the Truth

Instead, following the truth in love, let us grow in all things in him who is the head, that is, Christ. – Paul (Eph. 4:15)

Because truth is relative, many thinkers opt for the road of absolute negativism, making materialism an area of extreme intellectual perturbation.

How to interpret the truth if it seems to be so elusive to the ordinary methods of evaluation?

Boasting superiority, the officious scientist asserts that what is real does not go beyond organized forms, much like fanatics who only accept divine revelation within the circle of the dogmas they embrace.

Paul, however, offers a valuable suggestion to those who hope to enter the realm of higher understanding.

It is essential to follow the truth charitably, without the intent of incarcerating it in the cage of limited definition.

Let us convert the noble teachings we have received into love. Making an effort to combine truth with charity will result in spiritual progress. Unless we heed this imperative, we will run into strong obstacles on the path of sublimation. We need to grow in everything that life offers us that is useful and comely for an eternity with Christ; however, we will not be able to do so without daily transforming the small fragment of truth we possess into love for our neighbor.

Understanding asks for reality as much as reality asks for understanding.

Therefore, let us be truthful, but above all, let us be righteous.

~ 147 ~

It Is Not Solely That

But now rid yourselves of all these things: anger, rage, malice, slander and filthy language from your lips. – Paul (Col. 3:8)

In religious activity, many believe in moral reform in as much as the disciple of the faith remains unattached to certain material things.

Persons who hand out large amounts of clothing and food to the needy are regarded as being renewed in the Lord; however, even though this may be a form of true transformation, it does not represent the entirety of all the aspects related to the matter.

There are those who give away money on behalf of charity, but they do not budge from their personal opinion in an effort of sublime selflessness.

Enormous ranks of disciples proclaim their readiness to practice the good, but they insist on charitable work being carried out according to their own whims and not according to Jesus.

Everywhere, one hears fervent promises of faithfulness to Christ; however, no one can fulfill them without complying with all the necessary obligations.

A minor miscalculation in construction can upset the balance of an entire building. Thus, when people give some of their material possessions to help others, they should not forget to give up their old cloaks of rancor, prejudices, rash judgments or criminal frivolousness, so that they do not wear a heavy mask that makes them appear to be what they are not.

~ 148 ~

Harvesters

Then he said to his disciples, "The harvest is very great but there are few harvesters." (Mt. 9:37)

The lesson here does not refer to the spiritual harvest of the great periods of renewal throughout the ages, but rather the harvest of consolation that the Gospel enfolds within itself.

On the occasion referred to in Matthew, a crowd of disheartened and lost souls had gathered around the Master, like a flock without a shepherd. They were distraught faces and supplicant eyes displaying utter rejection.

At that point, Jesus used the symbol of a very great harvest accompanied by very few harvesters.

The Gospel is in the world as a blessed heavenly crop that is destined to enrich the human spirit; however, the percentage of individuals ready to take part in the harvest is quite small. Most await the beneficial wheat or the finished loaf for their own nourishment. Very rare are those who confront the storms, the rigors of the work and the dangerous surprises that the effort of harvesting requires of a devoted and faithful worker.

Thus, the multitude of the desperate and disillusioned has continued to walk the earth in increasing numbers down through the centuries.

The selfless workers of Christ have carried on, though overburdened due to the many hungry that surround the harvest without the courage to personally find the nourishment of life eternal for themselves. This picture will persist until good consumers also learn how to be good harvesters.

~ 149 ~

Believing in Vain

By this Gospel you are saved if you hold firmly to what I proclaimed to you; otherwise, you have believed in vain. – Paul (1 Cor. 15:2)

As with the many flowers that will not reach full bloom in the appropriate season, there are countless souls in the service of faith that do not achieve their own inner illumination after lifetimes of terrestrial struggle, having believed in vain along the paths of life.

Paul of Tarsus was very explicit when he assured the Corinthians that they would be saved if they held to the Gospel.

Jesus' revelation is an enormous field, with room for all humankind as far as areas of service are concerned.

Many arrive at the work site, but do not go beyond the written word, taking part in purely intellectual organizations. Some devise theological theories; some contribute to statistics, and others concern themselves with the historical placement of the Lord.

It is imperative to realize that every worthwhile task is useful at the proper time, depending on the sentiments of the worker; however, regarding the eternal life that Christianity unfolds before us, it is indispensable that we retain within ourselves the Master's teaching by focusing on applying it.

Each student ought to be a living page in the book that Jesus is writing with the evolutionary element of the earth. Disciples should engrave the Gospel on their own existence, or they will have to restart the learning experience once again, since without first setting the light of the lesson within them, they will have believed in vain.

~ 150 ~

He Is One and the Same

"Because the Father himself loves you." – Jesus (Jn. 16:27)

Let no one scorn the value of trust.

Let no servant flee from the benefit of being cooperative.

Whoever can give something useful today might have to require collaboration tomorrow.

However, even though someone becomes enriched with fraternity and faith, let him or her not forget the need to evolve infinitely in the good.

Earnest workers of the Gospel must act against pernicious favoritism.

The divine work has no privileged individuals. In its numerous areas, there are highly devoted and faithful workers; nevertheless, they should not be seen as objects of worship, but respected and imitated as symbols of loyalty and service.

Creating human idols is worse than worshiping statues. Marble is impassive, but the worker is our neighbor, whose status no one should abuse.

Let everyone pay the tribute of their own efforts to life.

The Supreme Lord expects only this of us in order to make us his direct collaborators.

Christ himself affirmed that the same Father who loves him loves all humankind equally.

The God who inspires the doctor is the same one who helps the sick.

It matters little if Asians and Europeans call God by different names.

Invariably, He is the same Father.

Let us therefore preserve the light of consolation, the blessing of fraternal assistance, and the trust in our Guides and Masters, assured of their watch-care. However, let us not forget that we have to use our own two feet to proceed towards the Most High.

~ 151 ~

No One Leaves

Simon Peter answered him, "Lord, to whom shall we go? You have the words of eternal life." (Jn. 6:68)

As the Master revealed new characteristics of his doctrine of love, his by-then-numerous followers began to understand their responsibilities more deeply. As a result, many of them grew afraid of their ensuing obligations and discreetly left the hospitable gathering of Capernaum.

Christ, however, was aware of the obligations of divine order, and rather than violating the principles of freedom, he assembled the small group that remained and asked his disciples:

"Do you too want to leave?"

This was the circumstance in which Peter gave his wise response, forever engraved in the Christian edifice.

The truth of the matter is that whoever begins the work of higher spirituality with Jesus will never again feel the same emotions when apart from him. The sublime experience may at times be interrupted, but it will never be destroyed. Compelled on various occasions by the demands of the physical realm, followers of the Gospel will suffer spiritual accidents that bring them briefly to a halt; however, they will not leave the pathway for good.

Whoever effectively partakes of the banquet of the Christian revelation will never forget the loving Master who sent them the invitation.

For this reason, Simon Peter asked fittingly:

"Lord, to whom shall we go?"

The world is replete with philosophers, scientists and reformers of all kinds, who are, of course, to be respected for the advanced human concepts they proclaim; but in most cases they are no more than simple expositors of transitory words that reflect fleeting experiences. Christ, however, is the Savior of souls and the Master of hearts, and in him we find the roads of life eternal.

~ 152 ~

In What Manner?

Which would you prefer? Shall I come to you with a whip or with love and a gentle spirit?
– Paul (1 Cor. 4:21)

At times, afire with sublime inspiration, the Apostle to the Gentiles addressed his brethren with direct questions that may seem almost mean if taken only literally, but which entail a wonderful reality when seen through the immortal light.

Vibrations of love and peace radiate in every Christian place. Jesus has never forsaken his faithful followers, no matter how far apart they may be on the terrain of interpretations.

Selfless emissaries of heavenly devotion have spread their sanctifying assistance throughout all the epochs of humankind. History demonstrates this as an irrefutable fact.

No century has ever lacked genuine missionaries of the good.

Promises and revelations from the Lord reach the ports of knowledge in a thousand ways.

In order to hide their personal failings, therefore, disciples who have joined the evangelical ranks cannot claim that they are unaware of the Gospel's objectives. Within the circle of their own responsibilities, each disciple has received the work plan to be carried out each day. If they run from the work and avoid bearing witness, they owe such an anomaly to their own inactive will.

Thus, it is possible that a time will come in which the idle and incessantly begging disciple may hear the Master personally and without any intermediaries, asking as Paul did:

"Which would you prefer? Shall I come to you with a whip, or with love and a gentle spirit?"

~ 153 ~

Let Us Not Stumble

Jesus answered, "Are there not twelve hours of daylight? If someone walks by day, he will not stumble, because he sees by this world's light."
(Jn. 11:9)

The content of this question by the Master has vast importance for today's disciples.

"Are there not twelve hours of daylight?"

Everyone should conscientiously ask themselves how they are using such a great wealth of time.

It is emphatically stressed that there is a problem with unemployment in modern times. However, any crisis of this nature is not the result of a lack of work, but rather of the absence of individual willingness.

A careful investigation would reveal the reality of the matter. Many individuals are idle because they rebel against the type of work that is offered to them, or because they object to the pay.

Imbalance immediately takes over.

When workers are idle, it attracts the attention of management, and the transitory laws of the world reflect animosity and distrust.

If hands stop working, factories come to a standstill.

The same occurs in the circles of spiritual activity.

How many disciples abandon their post, alleging they do not have time for it? How many become idle for this or that reason, in full disharmony with the superior principles they have embraced?

Because of trifles, large numbers of capable workers retreat into the shadows. However, those who have acute hearing can still listen profitably to the word of the Lord, "Are there not twelve hours of daylight? If someone walks by day, he will not stumble."

~ 154 ~

Those against Us

What shall we say in light of such things? If God is for us, who can be against us? – Paul (Rom. 8:31)

Paul's question still represents a beautiful theme for the evangelical community of today.

Awaiting our efforts, an immense field unfolds in which the Master looks for our resolute collaboration.

Frequently, however, many workers prefer to neglect the endeavor in order to squabble with evildoers along the way.

Adverse elements surround us everywhere.

Unexpected obstacles appear before our worried eyes; old friends leave us; yesterday's favorable situations metamorphose into cruel hostilities.

Huge ranks of workers flee from the peril, fearing the storm and forgetting about their witness.

However, we have not been given this work in order to surrender to panic, nor has the Master sent us to work with the objective of confusing us with external experiences.

We have been called upon to build.

Of course, we must expect a thousand eventualities each day that arise from opposing forces that make construction difficult. Our day of struggle will be besieged by troubles and fatigue. This is inevitable in a world that expects everything from the genuine Christian.

Due to this imperative, amid the threats and misunderstandings of the pathway, it is up to us to ask joyously like the Apostle to the Gentiles, "If God is for us, who can be against us?"

~ 155 ~

Against Foolishness

Are you so foolish that having begun in the spirit you have ended up in the flesh? – Paul (Gal. 3:3)

One of the greatest disasters on disciples' path is the erroneous understanding with which they begin their efforts in the higher spheres but end up reversing course toward the lower realms. Thus, they are like prospectors who start out looking for gold but wind up being content with the muck of the swampland.

Such failures are common in the various areas of religious thought.

We see patients who direct their thoughts to the higher realms, nourishing noble impulses and precious intentions; once healed, however, they think about the best way to use their newly-found health to acquire easy money. After being assisted by friends from the sublime spheres regarding the transcendental issues of eternal life, in their quest for unworthy objectives, they try to attribute to these same benefactors the role of human police.

Countless disciples persist in working for the good; however, when less favorable times appear, they passively yield to discouragement and demand a reward for the few years on earth in which they tried to serve in the harvest of the Divine Master. They completely overlook the many millennia in which they have been served by the Lord.

Such spiritual anomalies, which interfere greatly with disciples' efforts, originate from the poisonous filters composed of the strong desire for recompense.

Therefore, let us strive against the expectation of reward, so that in the company of humility – the bearer of the imperishable light – we may proceed with the task we have started.

~ 156 ~

Heaven upon Heaven

> *"But store up treasures in heaven, where neither moth nor rust consumes them, and where thieves cannot enter and steal them."* – Jesus (Mt. 6:20)

Within all Christian ranks, we encounter those ambitious for recompense, who think they have found in this statement by Jesus an effective recourse for retaliation against those who, through work and dedication, have received greater resources while on the earth.

What appears to be trust in God is actually disguised hatred for their fellow humans.

Because they have not been able to amass financial resources, they harbor critical and rebellious thoughts, waiting for their desired revenge in heaven.

However, it will not be through surrendering their body to the laboratory of nature that people will automatically find the realms of Resplendent Beauty.

Of course, imperishable sanctuaries shine in the sublime spheres, but one must remember that, in the spirit regions closest to human activity, there is still an immense number of moths and thieves in the evolutionary lines that extend beyond the grave.

When the Master recommended that we store up treasures in heaven, he was advising us to expand the virtues of the good in the peace of our hearts. Individuals who acquire faith and knowledge, virtue and illumination in the divine recesses of their conscience know the way to heaven. Those who apply the redemptive principles they embrace end up attaining this precious map; and those who work daily in the practice of the good continue to accumulate riches on the Peaks of Life.

Let no one be deceived about this.

Beyond the earth, the blessings of the Lord radiate in the Celestial Heights; however, one must possess light to perceive them.

The Law states that the Divine identifies with what is Divine, for no one can contemplate heaven by sheltering hell in their heart.

~ 157 ~

The Selfish Son

But in response he answered his father, "I have served you all these years and have never disobeyed one of your orders, yet you have never given me even a young goat so that I could celebrate with my friends." (Lk. 15:32)

This parable does not only introduce the prodigal son; if we look more closely, we also can see the selfish son.

The Master's veiled teaching displays two extremes of filial ingratitude. One resides in wastefulness; the other, in avarice. They are the two extremes that close the circle of human incomprehension.

Generally speaking, believers only see the son who abandoned his father's home in order to live in scandalous extravagance, hence deserving of every possible punishment. But few disciples have thought much about the condemnable conduct of the brother who remained under the family roof, and who was no less worthy of reprehension.

Upon seeing his father's generosity, the inferior sentiments that animate him rise to the surface in a display of selfishness.

The vibrations of love that reign in the domestic environment bother him. Like a truly lazy person, he refers to his years of service in the family; and like a prideful believer, he invokes his supposed observance of the Divine Law, and then disrespects his father because he is incapable of sharing in his well-founded joy.

This type of selfish individual is very common in the scenery of life. Faced with the well-being and happiness of others, they rebel and suffer because of the aridness that kills them and the jealousy that poisons them.

Reading the parable more closely, we do not know which son is the most unfortunate – the prodigal or the selfish one – but we would dare to believe in the immense unhappiness of the latter because the former already had the blessing of remorse in his favor.

~ 158 ~

Our Inner Government

I have subjugated my body and have reduced it to servitude so that in preaching to others, I myself may not in any way be reproved. – Paul (1 Cor. 9:27)

Actually, the body is a miniature of the Universe. It is indispensable, therefore, to know how to govern it.

As an earthly, material representation of the spirit's personality, it is reasonable for each one of us to pay attention to its dispositions. It is not that passive substance has more power than human will; however, it is imperative to realize that our inferior tendencies are intent on taking the power of control away from us.

It is crucial for each individual to be alert as to his or her self-governance.

The inner life in some ways resembles the life of a State. The spirit assumes self-control and is assisted by various ministries, such as the ministries of reflection, knowledge, understanding, respect and orderliness. Diverse and simultaneous thoughts comprise good or bad appeals from our inner parliament. In the depths of each mind there is broad potential for progress and sublimation, but it requires work.

As supreme governor of the cellular cosmos, the spirit issues beneficial laws but it does not always mobilize the monitoring organs of its own will. The inferior zones continue their previous disorder, disregarding renewing decrees that they neither defy nor carry out. When this anomaly occurs, the individual actually becomes a living enigma, if not a blind or evil person.

Whoever expects to live a healthy life without self-discipline is not far from ruinous or complete imbalance.

It is necessary to implement our self-governance in every position in life. The fundamental issue resides in a strong will toward ourselves, and goodwill toward our brothers and sisters.

~ 159 ~

Possessing the Kingdom

Strengthening the disciples' courage, exhorting them to remain in the faith, and saying that we must go through much tribulation to enter the Kingdom of God. (Acts 14:22)

The Gospel deceives no one about what it teaches.

The preoccupation of believers trying to bribe the divine forces is quite common. However, it will not be at the price of many masses, hymns or psychic sessions that people will accomplish the sublime acquisition of lofty spirituality.

Of course, all spiritually constructive practice is a helpful element; however, each human being is responsible for his or her own efforts at illumination.

The Good News does not hand out indulgences at the world's price, and the individual can find many, many pathways that lead upward.

There are many places of worship and teachers, and each one offers a bit of help or assistance in the service of spiritual guidance. However, to enter and take possession of the eternal inheritance will occur through righteous witness.

This is not accidental. It is a necessary and logical measure.

Rare statues are not created without the blows of the chisel, nor is wheat harvested without the soil having been tilled.

More than a few disciples interpret certain warnings in the Gospel as an excessive exhortation to suffering; however, what appears to them to be an obsession with pain is actually an imperative for the education of the soul for life eternal.

No one will ever find the infinite estuary of the divine energies without the aid of earthly tribulations.

A person without struggle on the earth is a narrow soul. Only work and self-sacrifice, difficulties and obstacles as elements for progress and personal improvement can give the individual a truthful assessment of his or her greatness.

~ 160 ~

The Great Struggle

We do not have to struggle against flesh and blood, but against principalities, against powers, against the princes of the darkness of this age, and against spiritual hosts of wickedness in heavenly places. – Paul (Eph. 6:12)

According to what we have said time and again, the great struggle does not actually reside in the fight with blood and flesh per se, but rather with our own inferior spiritual dispositions.

Paul of Tarsus was divinely inspired when he wrote this recommendation to his brethren at Ephesus.

The silent and incessant conflict between earnest disciples and the forces of darkness is linked to our own personal nature, for we were willing accomplices of evil in the not-too-distant past.

We have been declared participants in unlawful actions in heavenly places.

And even today, amongst the condensed fluids of the flesh or in the spheres closest to them, we are involved in the work of self-restoration in the midst of paradise.

The earth too is also a sublime stepping stone of heaven.

When someone refers to fallen angels, human listeners immediately imagine a magnificent, mysterious palace, from which wise and luminous beings were expelled.

But does not the same thing happen when an educated individual turns into a murderer in front of a university or a house of worship?

Generally, the earthly witness reports the crime; however, he or she does not stop to analyze the sacred and venerable place where it occurred.

The great struggle the Apostle refers to has continued without pause.

Cities and human constructions are zones of heaven. Neither they nor the organic cells that serve us are powerful enemies, but rather "the spiritual hosts of wickedness," with which we attune ourselves through the inferior links we desperately hold on to: vast groups of beings and somber thoughts that obscure human vision, and which act subtly so as not to lose their industrious companions of yesterday.

~ 161 ~

But You, What do You Say?

And he asked them, "But you, who do you say I am?" (Lk. 9:20)

In discussions proper to the world, there will always be writers and scientists ready to examine the Master according to the guidelines of their purely intellectual impressions from the perspective of human presumption.

But these friends have not had contact with the soul of the Gospel. They have not gone beyond academic circles, nor have they risked their conventional titles on a dispassionate excursion into divine revelation; so of course they will continue to be deceived by the vanity, prejudice or fear that is typical of their transitory manner of being until their lives are renewed on the paths of life everlasting.

Nonetheless, within sincere and faithful disciples, the question posed by Jesus takes on singular importance.

Each one of us should have our own personal opinions regarding the wisdom and mercy with which we have been blessed.

Meaningless conversations regarding the Christ are suitable only for spirits disoriented on the road of life. We, however, are responsible for our inner testimony to the Lord because we are direct beneficiaries of his infinite goodness. Let us meditate and renew our aspirations according to his Gospel of Love, recognizing the impropriety of mutual interpellations with respect to the Master, for the sublime question comes from him to each one of us and we must all know him in order to incorporate him into our daily chores.

~ 162 ~

Spirit Manifestations

But the manifestation of the spirit is given to each one for whatever is useful. – Paul (1 Cor. 12:7)

With the revival of pure Christianity in Spiritist groups following Jesus, the same concern that afflicted the disciples in apostolic times with regards to mediumship is still present.

The majority of workers involved in evangelization are overly eager for the immediate development of incipient mediumship faculties.

At certain Spiritist centers, achievements beyond the mediums' current abilities are expected; at others, impressive phenomena are dreamed about.

The issue, however, cannot be summed up in acquisitions from the outside.

As individuals develop their own inner illumination and intensify their spiritual powers through knowledge and love, they will enter into the possession of eternal treasures in a natural way.

Motivated by expectations of superiority, many disciples would like to be great seeing mediums or admirable revealers; however, they do not bother to consider the effort needed for such a sublime achievement.

They desire the gains but do not think about the hard work. In this regard, it is important to remember that Simon Peter, whose spirit felt so attuned to the glorious Master on Tabor, could not bear the anguish of his Friend tortured on Calvary.

It is right for disciples to aspire to grow spiritually; however, those possessing a humble mediumistic faculty should not disdain it simply because someone else possesses more ostensible qualities. Let each and every one work with the material they have been entrusted with, knowing that in the matter of spirit manifestations the Supreme Lord does not provide them according to human whims, but according to their overall usefulness.

~ 163 ~

Be Thankful

And be thankful. – Paul (Col. 3:15)

It is curious to note that a lot of disciples are always interested in receiving blessings, but it is quite rare to find someone who is willing to render them.

However, in their normal use, spiritual resources should obey the same system applied to provisions of a material order.

As far as the soul's blessings are concerned, they should not be received and spent foolishly, but prudently and rightly so that their potential is not absorbed by disorder and injustice.

Consequently, in his instructions to the Christians at Colossae, the apostle recommends that we be thankful.

Among earnest disciples, the old habit of expressing thanks in bombastic and obsequious words is not justified. In the community of workers loyal to Jesus, to be thankful means to usefully employ the blessings received as much for our neighbors as for ourselves.

For loving parents, the best thanks from their children consist in the high-level understanding of work and life to which they attest.

Expressing their gratitude to Christ, his apostles were so faithful to him that they made the ultimate sacrifice; Paul of Tarsus received the call from the Master and in a display of happiness and love, he served the Divine Cause through indescribable suffering for more than thirty years.

Being thankful does not mean only the utterance of fine-sounding words; rather, it means feeling the greatness of gestures, the light of benefits received, the generosity of trust, and willingly extending to others the treasures of life.

~ 164 ~

The Devil

Jesus answered him, "Have I not chosen you, the Twelve? Yet, one of you is a devil. (Jn. 6:70)

When theology refers to the Devil, the believer immediately imagines the lord of absolute evil, dominating an endless hell.

In a disciple's way of thinking, the region of evil is located in a distant sphere, in the heart of tormenting darkness...

Of course, the purgatorial zones are numerous and somber, terrible and painful, but according to Jesus' own affirmation, the Devil took part in the apostolic work, and one of the disciples would represent the infernal spirit himself. This is enough for us to realize that the term "the Devil," in the Master's way of thinking, does not refer to a powerful and eternal giant of wickedness in space and time. It refers to humans themselves while chained to the turpitudes of the lower sentiments.

Hence, we must conclude that each person displays a certain percentage of diabolical tendencies in the inferior aspect of his or her personality.

Satan thus symbolizes the power that is contrary to the good.

When humans discover evil in the vast world of themselves, they understand it, fight against it, avoid their inner hell and develop the divine qualities that elevate them to a higher level of spirituality.

Large multitudes have been immersed in desperation for hundreds of years for not having been able to grasp this truth.

And commenting on this passage from John, we must consider: "If among the twelve apostles there was one that became a devil in spite of the divine mission of the circle destined to transform the world, how many exist in each group of ordinary men and women?"

~ 165 ~

False Speech

But be fulfillers of the word and not just hearers, deceiving yourselves with false speech. (Js. 1:22)

It is never too much to comment on the importance and sacred character of speech.

The Gospel itself affirms that in the beginning was the Word, and whoever closely examines the current state of the world today will realize that every problematic situation was caused by a poor application of the power of the word.

False speech has deceived individuals, families and nations. Some have believed in vain promises; others, in fallacious theories, and still others, in prospects of freedom without responsibility. Upon realizing the deception, nations, groups and individuals antagonize one another, seeking to determine culpability.

The human word has cost much blood and many tears. At present, it would be impossible to compute this dreadful price or determine the amount of time it would take to pay it in full.

In the whirlwind of struggles, however, followers of Christ can take advantage of the treasure of the gospel for their individual benefit.

To comply with the word of the Master within us is the divine plan. Without implementing this plan of salvation, the other work under our responsibility will constitute sublimated theology, brilliant lectures, magnificent literature, and much admiration and respect on the lower field of the world, but never the required accomplishment.

That is the reason why it is always dangerous to stop along the way to listen to those who have fled the reality of their duties.

~ 166 ~

The Cure for Hatred

Therefore, if your enemy is hungry, give him to eat; if he is thirsty, give him to drink, for in doing so, you will heap coals of fire on his head. – Paul (Rom. 12:20)

When individuals decide to serve the good, they usually encounter ranks of gratuitous adversaries wherever they go, as invariably occurs to the light besieged by the enmity of the darkness.

Sometimes, however, whether due to errors in their past or incomprehension in the present, they are confronted by more powerful enemies who become a constant menace to their tranquility. To have enemies of this kind is to endure a painful inner infirmity if the individual has not yet given living witness to the Gospel.

Usually, disciples of goodwill will do everything they can for reconciliation; nevertheless, the greatest efforts might seem futile. Impenetrability characterizes the heart of the other, and the best gestures of love go unnoticed.

To counter this situation, however, the Divine Book offers a healthy recipe. It is not advisable to aggravate differences or to incite quarrels, and the well-intentioned individual should never resort to flattery. Wait for the proper opportunity to manifest the good.

From the minute in which the offended person forgets the discord and moves back to love, the service of Jesus is restored; however, the offender's perception might be slower, and in many occasions, he or she only understands the new light when it can be seen as personal gain.

Sincere disciples of Christ more easily free themselves from their inferior bonds, whereas yesterday's antagonists can persist for a long time in the hardness of their hearts. That is why doing good to them at the right moment is to heap the renewing fire on their heads, curing the infernal displays of their hatred.

~ 167 ~

Understanding

Be transformed by the renewing of your understanding. – Paul (Rom. 12:2)

When we refer to the issue of spiritual transformation, the community of disciples of the Gospel agrees with us as to its necessity, but not all express a perfect understanding of the matter.

Deep down, they all yearn to change, but most only aspire to conventional change.

Those less fortunate monetarily seek to scale the realm of material possibilities, while the holders of humble jobs strive for higher positions, and in a disconcerting crescendo, nearly all plan the unfounded transformation of the opportunities at hand, immersing themselves in disquieting disorder. Indispensable renewal does not involve the fluctuating outer plane. Devoted Christians will not be transformed outwardly, but rather through understanding, endowing their own minds with new light, new concepts.

Just as any earthly job requires that workers sincerely apply themselves to it, the job of mental growth requires constant effort in the good and knowledge.

Even here, it is important to realize that discipline will be a decisive factor.

Therefore, do not become crystallized in wrongful ideas that have harmed you in the past.

Be attentive to the structure of your reasoning today in light of the circumstances that surround you. Ask yourself how much understanding you have gained from the Gospel so that you can correctly analyze this or that incident on your path. Do this and the Goodness of the Lord will assist you in the enlightening reply to yourself.

~ 168 ~

At Dawn

And on the first day of the week, Mary Magdalene went to the tomb while it was still dark, and saw that the stone had been rolled away. (Jn. 20:1)

We must not forget the circumstance in which Mary Magdalene receives the first message regarding the Master's resurrection.

Amid the troubles and discouragement of her small group, the great convert wastes no time on pointless grief, nor does she seek the sleep of forgetfulness.

Her companions had lost their faith. Between remorse for their own desertion and their sorrow for the sacrifice of the Savior – whose sublime lesson they still had not managed to grasp – they had become confused in negative attitudes. Contradictory and anguishing thoughts pierced their hearts.

Magdalene, however, rends the veil of grief that hinders her steps. It is crucial not to be crushed under burdens, but to make them an essential element of spiritual growth, so Mary resolves not to cower in the face of sorrow. Since Christ had been immolated on the cross, it would not be right to condemn his beloved memory to oblivion or indifference.

Watchful and attentive to her objective, rather than giving in to old conventions, she leaves very early in the morning to confront the great obstacle, the tomb. In doing so, she precedes the awakening of her own friends and finds the radiant answer of Life Eternal.

As we recall this symbolic event, let us remember our old failures, for having forgotten the "first day of the week," for having exchanged, on every occasion, the "very early" for the "very late."

~ 169 ~

Eyes

Their eyes are full of adultery. (2 Pet. 2:14)

"Eyes full of adultery" constitute a rebellious malady in our evolutionary struggles.

Rare are those who use their eyes as blessed lanterns, and few are those who use them as living instruments for sanctifying work.

Most people use them to spot the worst in whatever situation they find themselves.

Ordinary people usually look at a certain situation only to determine the angles most advantageous to their inferior interests. If they cross a field, they do not make note of its beneficent function for society, but the potential for the personal and immediate gain it might offer. If men meet an affable sister on the human path, they frequently scheme dishonorable connections. If they run into their friends in places where they themselves have come to fulfill their unworthy intentions, they do not recognize them as possible bearers of elevated ideas, but as competitors of their own unfortunate plans.

Let us heed Simon Peter's cry of alarm and put aside the habit of studying a situation with an eye on evil.

Optimistic eyes know how to extract sublime teachings from the most diverse situations on their path.

Let no one invoke the need to be watchful just so they can justify manifestations of malice. Prudent Christians recognize their own problems, but they never see evil where evil does not exist.

~ 170 ~

The Tongue

The tongue is also a fire. (Js. 3:6)

People's indifference justifies James's stern considerations in his epistle to his fellow disciples.

The origin of all the adversity on the planet is nearly always located in the misuse of the tongue.

The great Apostle of Jerusalem reminds them that the tongue has been placed among the other parts of the body as the helm of a powerful ship.

Within its potentiality there are sacred elements of creation, and like a small helm, it was installed to steer.

The tongue holds the divine spark of the word; however, people usually divert it from its edifying function and place it in the swamp of subaltern thoughts. This is why we see it at the forefront of nearly all the folly of suffering humankind, which is dead set on its petty objectives that lack humility and love.

War is born from the language of unsatisfied criminal interests. Great societal tragedies are often caused by conversation based on inferior sentiments.

People's tongues have seldom consoled or edified their brothers and sisters; instead, they are always ready to excite, argue, depress, slander, accuse and harm mercilessly.

The sincere disciple will find in James's statements a brilliant application for every experience. And when night falls at the end of each day, it is fitting to ask oneself: "Have I used my tongue today as Jesus used his?"

~ 171 ~

The Law of Usage

When they were filled, Jesus said to his disciples: "Gather the pieces that are left over so that nothing is wasted." (Jn. 6:12)

When the law of usage is finally observed, misery will flee the human path.

To counter waste and avarice, everyone must contribute, because once balance is established, the endeavor of economic justice will be complete as long as goodwill dwells with all.

This passage from the Gospel describes the task of feeding the multitude. It points out the important words of the Lord with regards to the leftover bread, and thus transmits a teaching of profound significance to the disciples.

Generally speaking, in the first dazzling light of revelatory faith, sincere disciples want to be profuse in charitable activities, but without any basis in true harmony.

This is inarguably a laudable impulse, but even in the distribution of material goods one must avoid excess and lack of control.

The Father does not eliminate winter because some of his children complain about the cold, but he does equalize the situation by giving them warm clothing.

Charity calls for enthusiasm; however, it also requires generous discernment, which does not incline the heart to indifference.

In the large gathering of the needy on the mount, there was certainly no lack of lazy and prodigal persons who were ready to needlessly waste the rest of the bread. However, before such careless individuals appeared, Jesus recommended clearly: "Gather the pieces that are left over so that nothing is wasted." Thus, in all things, people should realize that usage is part of the Law, thus discouraging waste, which is deadly poison in the springs of life.

~ 172 ~

What Do You Awaken?

Thus they were carrying the sick into the streets and were laying them on cots and mats so that Peter's shadow might at least fall on some of them as he passed by. (Acts 5:15)

Conquerors of bloody glories spread terror and ruin wherever they go.

Shrewd politicians sow distrust and doubt.

The biased judge awakens harmful fear.

The rebel spreads clouds of subtle poison.

Gossipers instill an evil disposition in their listeners, causing pernicious rumors.

Slanderers send out threads of darkness on their path.

Lazy persons sap the strength of those they meet, injecting them with numbing fluids.

Liars leave trouble and insecurity wherever they go.

With their mere presence, jesters inspire and encourage funny tales.

All of us, through thoughts, words and actions, create a distinct atmosphere that identifies us in the eyes of others.

The shadow of Simon Peter, who had accepted the Christ and had dedicated himself to him, was sought after by the suffering and the sick, who found hope and relief, comfort and joy in it.

Examine the topics and attitudes that your presence awakens in others. Pay attention and you will discover the quality of your shadow, and if you are interested in acquiring illuminative qualities with Jesus, it will be easy for you to discover your deficiencies and correct them.

~ 173 ~

How To Bear Witness

But you will receive the power of the Holy Spirit, who shall come upon you; and you will be my witnesses both in Jerusalem and in all Judea and Samaria, and even to the ends of the earth. (Acts 1:8)

Truly, Jesus is the Savior of the World, but he will not deliver it from the control of evil without the contribution of those who seek his saving resources.

The Divine Master, therefore, needs collaborators to act as agents and witnesses everywhere.

The development of souls is unfeasible without education, and education requires legions of workers.

However, in order for us to perform the role of the Lord's representatives in the sublime endeavor of spiritual growth, the outward titles of a religious creed are not enough.

It is indispensable to receive blessings from On High by carrying out our duties, no matter how difficult and painful they may be.

Up until now, we have fully known the power to dominate, to rule, to refuse and to injure: all these find easy access to the arena of life.

But few individuals work to deserve from Jesus the heavenly power of obedience by teaching, of loving by building for the good, of waiting by working, and of assisting unselfishly. Without receiving such resources, which identify us with the Divine Worker, and without having the ability to reflect him for our neighbor in spirit and truth through our constant effort to apply the Gospel to ourselves, we can embody excellent preachers, brilliant literary men and women, or noteworthy sympathizers of the Christian Doctrine, but we cannot be his witnesses.

~ 174 ~

Spiritism in the Faith

> *"And these signs will accompany those who believe: In my name they will drive out demons; they will speak in new tongues." – Jesus (Mk. 16:17)*

Within the most varied spheres of the faith, manifestations of the spirit life exist in all the fundamentals of the Divine Revelation.

Spiritism per se, therefore, ceases to be a novelty in our times; rather, it is at the root of all the branches of religion.

Moses establishes contact with the spirit realm on Mt. Sinai.

Jesus is seen by the disciples on Mt. Tabor flanked by illustrious deceased personalities.

The apostolic community has an ongoing relationship with the Master's spirit after his death, and consolidates redemptive Christianity in the world.

The martyrs in the Roman arenas abandon their flagellated flesh as they contemplate sublime visions.

Mohammed initiates his religious endeavor upon hearing an invisible messenger.

Francis of Assisi perceives emissaries from Heaven, who exhort him to renew the Church.

Luther registers the presence of beings from the other world.

Teresa of Avila receives the visit of discarnate friends and even goes to the purgatorial regions through the mediumistic out-of-the-body phenomenon.

Christ affirms that signs from the spirit realm will accompany those who believe. In all institutions of faith, there are those who enjoy, who make use of, who calculate, who criticize, who oversee ... Even these are candidates for decisive, renewing illumination. However, those who believe and accept the work orders that flow down from On High will be accompanied by the revelatory signs of immortality wherever they may be at the time. By emitting sanctifying vibrations in the Lord's name, they will cast out darkness and evil, and will be easily recognized by amazed men and women because they will always speak in the new language of sacrifice, peace, selflessness and love.

~ 175 ~

Treating Obsession

Many people gathered from the towns around Jerusalem, bringing the sick and those tormented by evil spirits, and all were healed.
(Acts 5:16)

The early Christian church did not smother the redemptive ideas of Christ in the silver and splendors of outward worship.

It was alive, full of appeals and answers.

Similarly, evangelical Spiritism today opens its benevolent doors to those who suffer and seek the way of salvation.

It is interesting to note that today's Spiritists' enormous task providing relief for complex and dolorous obsessions was very well known by the apostles. They counseled troubled spirits, regenerating not only discarnate sufferers through example and instruction, but also the afflicted mediums who were suffering under their influence.

From the very start of the doctrinal endeavor, the soul of Christianity has known that imbalanced, invisible beings roam the world, causing psychic wounds in those who receive their influence. Moreover, it is fully aware of the demanding work of conversion and spiritual elevation that it has been called to perform. Religious dogmas, however, have kept it from working effectively for many centuries.

Nowadays, however, the early scenes of the Good News have resurfaced.

Ignorant and unfortunate spirits receive a new light and a new direction in the centers of love that Christian Spiritism has established, thereby overcoming deep-set prejudices and difficulties.

The treatment of obsession, therefore, is not an eccentric endeavor in our spheres of regenerative faith. It is simply the continuation of the effort of saving wayward souls of all sorts, which began with the luminous hands of Jesus.

~ 176 ~

In the Revelation of Life

And with great power the apostles bore witness to the resurrection of the Lord Jesus, and amongst all of them there was abundant grace. (Acts 4:33)

The direct companions of the Divine Master did not establish the work of the Christian community upon crystallized, inflexible principles. They cultivated order, hierarchy and discipline, but they also assisted the spirit of the people by distributing the goods of spiritual revelation according to the receptive ability of each one of the aspirants to the new faith.

At present, to use the name of the Christian Faith to deny the authenticity of the Spiritist endeavor is evidence of either ignorance or thoughtlessness.

The Lord's disciples understood the importance of the certainty of life after death in order to triumph in the moral life. They themselves were radically transformed after the resurrection of their Heavenly Friend upon realizing that love and justice govern the individual in the afterlife. For this very reason, they attracted new followers, transmitting to them their conviction that the Master continued to live and work beyond the tomb.

Consequently, the apostolic ministry was not divided solely into discussing the intellectual problems of the faith and involving itself in worshipful praise. "With great power" Christ's followers "bore witness to the resurrection of the Lord Jesus," and because of the love with which they devoted themselves to the work of salvation, amongst them there was "abundant grace."

Evangelical Spiritism has set in motion the divine work, which entails not only consoling faith but also the indisputable knowledge of immortality.

Dogmatic Christian denominations will continue holding to articles of inoperative faith, thereby freezing their minds in absurd affirmations; however, in its redemptive activities, Christian Spiritism has come to restore the teaching of the resurrection of the individual, a teaching consecrated by the Divine Master, who returned from the shadows of death personally in order to extol the continuity of life.

~ 177 ~

Let Us Guard Our Mental Health

"Think on things that are above and not on those that are of the earth." – Paul (Col. 3:2)

Early Christianity was fully aware of the need for a sound mind enlightened by higher aspirations in the lives of those who embraced the Gospel for their inner reform.

The work of notable present-day thinkers finds its roots much earlier.

Nowadays, those who deal with mediumistic phenomena know that the death of the flesh does not entail the delights of heaven.

Beyond the grave, individuals find themselves with all the virtues and defects, ideas and vices they sanctioned while in the body.

Criminals are drawn to the arena of their crimes if they are not shackled to their accomplices.

Misers are bound to the superfluous wealth they wantonly hoarded.

The vain remain tied to their fleeting titles.

Alcoholics make the rounds, looking to satisfy the thirst that controls their energy centers.

Those who surrendered to the lower whims of the "self" spend many days trying to undo the webs of illusion in which their personality is segregated.

The plan comes before the work.

The project maps out its implementation.

Thought is a radiating energy. If we concentrate it on the earth, we will naturally bind ourselves to the ground. If we lift it On High, we will enter the sublime spirit realms.

Our spirit will reside wherever we project our thoughts, the living bases of both good and evil. For this very reason Paul stated wisely, "Think on things that are above."

~ 178 ~

The Inner Struggle

"Having the same struggle that you saw I had, and which you have heard that I still have." – Paul (Phil. 1:30)

In his youth, Paul fought against ordinary circumstances in order to consolidate his position and assert himself in the future of his people. He strove to surpass the intelligence of many of his contemporaries, leaving colleagues and friends far behind. He argued with doctors of the Law and won. He threw himself into winning an enviable material situation and succeeded. He endeavored to prove himself in the highest court of Jerusalem and surpassed the elders of the chosen people. He decided to persecute those he regarded as enemies of the established order, and multiplied enemies all around him. He wounded, tormented and complicated the situations of respectable friends; he sentenced innocent people to indescribable tribulations and he waged war against sinners and saints, the righteous and the wicked...

However, a moment came in which the Lord called his spirit to another type of struggle: the struggle with himself.

When that time arrives, Paul of Tarsus becomes silent and listens…

The sword breaks in his hands forever.

He no longer has hands that attack, but that help and serve.

He proceeds, transformed, in reverse. Instead of humiliating others, he bows his head.

He suffers and perfects himself in silence with the same disposition for work that characterized him in his times of blindness.

He is stoned, whipped and imprisoned; he is often misunderstood, but he continues onward towards the encounter with the Divine Renewal.

If you do not yet struggle with yourself, the day will come when you will be called to such a task. Pray and be watchful; prepare yourself and adapt your heart to humility and patience. My brothers and sisters, remember that not even Paul, who was blessed by a personal visit from Jesus, managed to escape.

~ 179 ~

Let Us Understand by Serving

Because we too were once foolish. – Paul (Titus 3:3)

The hammer certainly takes part in perfecting the sculpture, but it cannot beat the stone indiscriminately.

The bitter medicine may heal a sick body, but knowing the correct dosage is required.

No more, no less.

It is also crucial for us not to act impulsively in the sowing of truth.

While on the earth, we do not live in a dwelling for angels.

We comprise millions of individuals in a maze of clamorous past debts, yearning for deliverance.

Those who teach with sincerity have learned their lessons after having overcome difficult obstacles.

Of course, excessive tolerance results in an absence of just defense; however, it cannot be denied that in order to educate others, we need a great deal of patience and understanding.

Incisive and forceful, Paul was fully aware of this fact.

Writing to Titus, he recalls his own incomprehension in the past in order to justify the peace-of-mind that should characterize our work in the service of the Redemptive Gospel.

We will never reach our objectives by tormenting others' wounds, by pointing out their scars, by commenting on their defects, or by throwing thorns in their face.

Understanding and respect must precede our work everywhere.

Let us remember our own passage through the lower realms, and let us extend our fraternal arms to our brothers and sisters struggling in the darkness.

If you are interested in taking part in Christ's work, remember that He did not act from the prosecutor's office, but from the tribunal of sacrifice on the cross as the attorney for the whole entire world.

~ 180 ~

Believe and Press On

"Just as you sent me into the world, I have sent them into the world." – Jesus (Jn. 17:18)

My friend, if you have embraced the Christian Spiritist task in the name of the sublime faith, thirsting for a more uplifting spiritual life, remember that the Master has sent your renewed soul to the vast field of the world in order to serve Him.

You are not only to teach the way of the good. You are to act in accordance with the lofty principles that you proclaim.

You are to dictate worthy directives to others, but you are to heed them as well.

You are to proclaim the need for courage while sowing joy and blessings even when you are misunderstood by all.

You are not to be content with simply handing out coins and immediate relief. You are to always give a bit of yourself to whomever is in need.

You are to not only forgive; you are to understand the offender, helping him or her to get up.

You are not to criticize. You are to find unexpected ways to be useful.

You are not to yell. You are to make use of time in order to materialize the good thoughts that guide you.

You are not to argue needlessly. You are to find a way to serve others wherever you are.

You are not to merely combat evil with words. You are to preserve the good, sharing it with everyone.

You are not to condemn. You are to discover the light of love in order to make it shine in your heart until death.

Pray and watch.

Love and wait.

Serve and deny yourself.

If you are not willing to apply the Divine Master's lesson to your own life, your faith will have been useless.

16124995R00216

Made in the USA
Charleston, SC
06 December 2012